Accepting God's Invitation
to a More Fulfilling Life

——— A ———
GENEROUS
BECKONING

PETER M. WALLACE

Library of Congress Control Number: 2022944163

Versions of some of these meditations appeared in an earlier book written by the author entitled *Out of the Quiet*.

#2644

978-0-88028-510-0

Forward
Movement
inspire disciples. empower evangelists.

Accepting God's Invitation
to a More Fulfilling Life

A
GENEROUS
BECKONING

PETER M. WALLACE

FORWARD MOVEMENT
Cincinnati, Ohio

Dedication

For five dear Episcopal priests who have
mentored and inspired me over the years:
the Rev. Canon Gray Temple, Jr.,
the Rev. Canon Louis C. "Skip" Schueddig,
the Rev. James Hagen,
the Rev. Allan Sandlin, and
the Rev. Canon Scott Gunn.
They represent countless others who have
enriched my life deeply and helped to form me
as a priest and as a human..

Contents

Contents

Contents

Contents

God woos us with…
A Generous Beckoning

Introduction

Listening for God's Invitations in Three Dimensions

What Is God Saying to You?

Elijah was scared to death. The prophet's bold proclamations had gotten him in big trouble with the powers that be, and a furious Queen Jezebel had put a generous price on his head.

For forty days and forty nights, Elijah ran for his life all the way to the mountain of God, Mount Horeb, where he collapsed, exhausted, in a cave. And slept.

> At that place he came to a cave, and spent the night there. Then the word of the LORD came to him, saying, "What are you doing here, Elijah?" He answered, "I have been very zealous for the LORD, the God of hosts; for the Israelites have forsaken your covenant, thrown down your altars, and killed your prophets with the sword. I alone am left, and they are seeking my life, to take it away." He said, "Go out and stand on the

mountain before the LORD, for the LORD is about to pass by." Now there was a great wind, so strong that it was splitting mountains and breaking rocks in pieces before the LORD, but the LORD was not in the wind; and after the wind an earthquake, but the LORD was not in the earthquake; and after the earthquake a fire, but the LORD was not in the fire; and after the fire a sound of sheer silence. When Elijah heard it, he wrapped his face in his mantle and went out and stood at the entrance of the cave. Then there came a voice to him that said, "What are you doing here, Elijah?" (1 Kings 19:9-13)

You may not be holed up in a cave in the wilderness, but you may feel a lot like Elijah.

Running for your life.

Exhausted by the seemingly perpetual battle for survival in this world.

Aching for God's presence.

Frustrated that you have done so many of the right things with so little to show for it except heartache.

Yearning to hear the voice of God for you.

And wondering, "What are you doing here?"

Sometimes, God's message for you is right there in front
of you: a quiet whisper, the "sound of sheer silence," easily
ignored, easy to overlook.

My goal in these pages is to help you listen carefully for what
God is saying to you today, what God is inviting into your life.
As we journey together through a variety of texts throughout
the Bible, each springing from a verb in the imperative case,
I hope we will train our spiritual ears and eyes to see God
beckoning generously to us, ever coaxing us to come closer,
inviting us to experience life in all its fullness.

The Bible is soaked through and through with God's desire
to bring us closer into a divine, loving embrace. In a meeting
of an interfaith association once, I heard a Muslim woman
quote a verse from the *Hadith Qudsi*, the sayings of Prophet
Muhammed, in which God says:

> "If he draws near to Me a hand's span, I draw near to
> him an arm's length; and if he draws near to Me an
> arm's length, I draw near to him a fathom's length. And
> if he comes to Me walking, I go to him running."[1]

God in Three Persons yearns for you.

Jesus expresses anguish over the folks who seem to have no
interest in the lavish gifts he wants to share:

> For this people's heart has grown dull, and their ears
> are hard of hearing, and they have shut their eyes; so

that they might not look with their eyes, and listen with their ears, and understand with their heart and turn—and I would heal them. (Matthew 13:15)

Beloved sibling, Jesus wants to heal you. Fill you. Embrace you. Share with you. Encourage you. Challenge you. But you must be alert to his invitations to come and follow.

It all starts with listening, really listening, for what God is saying to you. Right from the pages of the Bible.

What Are You Saying to God?

Whether you're a seeker taking initial steps in your pursuit of God, or you've been a Christian for many years but desire a fresh, true encounter with God in your daily life, this book offers you opportunities to hear and wrestle with God's imperatives—invitations, admonitions, challenges, and commands—to you.

This book will have the most benefit to you if you are earnestly seeking the kind of help it offers. That is, you have certain needs you want fulfilled—and you're asking God to fulfill them:

"God, I want to hear you."

Perhaps you are feeling frustrated because there is a disconnect between God's Word and your daily life. You live in a world whose distracting roar keeps you from hearing the "sheer sound of silence" of God's presence. It seems you can't hear God speaking personally to you, so you fail to achieve the spiritual potential God has for you.

This book is designed to enable you to hear God speak to you through powerful passages from the Old and New Testaments, and to help you grasp the full magnitude of what God's imperatives can mean to you as a child of God.

"God, I want to experience you more fully in my daily life."

The Bible is a big book full of stories and teachings for God's children to read, understand, and follow—or, as Episcopalians like to say, to hear, read, mark, learn, and inwardly digest. It takes a lifetime to interact with the Bible, to apply it, and to live it.

This book will help you focus on God's words to you, so you can come to know God better and accept the invitation to a deeper, richer, more authentic relationship with God in Three Persons:

Father, Son, Holy Spirit

Creator, Redeemer, Sustainer

Source, Savior, Sanctifier

Lover, Beloved, Love[2]

Holy Parent, Divine Child, Breath of God

"God, I want meditations that don't tell me what to believe but introduce me to you and your word and help me work it out myself."

You and I are on this journey together. We are continually trying to figure out how best to relate with God and each other. We are seeking to experience God more genuinely and then to share that experience with each other.

So together, we'll interact with invitations to you from the Father, the Creator, in the Old Testament. We'll explore the admonitions to you from the Son, the Redeemer, in the gospels. And we will look at the urgings to you from the Holy Spirit, the Sustainer, in the New Testament Epistles. And I hope when we're done, we'll both realize how much closer we've grown to God.

How Can This Book Enliven the Conversation?

This is a book of meditations. This means we won't be studying scholarly theories about Bible passages or debating fine points of theology. We won't be sidetracked by historical timelines or authorship controversies. Rather, we're taking God's Word as we've received it at face value. We're interacting personally—emotionally, intellectually, and spiritually—with what we read there. We're inviting the Spirit to help us sense the grace, love, and power of God.

You can read *A Generous Beckoning* straight through at any pace. Or you can focus on one devotional segment each day.

Or browse the contents page to find a particular topic that speaks to you on any given day.

When you begin to hear God speaking to you in the scripture, communicating directly to you in commands and invitations and admonitions, then you start to enter into a deeper relationship with God through the Spirit who woos you. You will experience a more authentic spirituality. You'll no longer simply go through the motions or feel too tired or lazy to make the effort and spend the time to pray or read the scripture. Instead, you'll grow increasingly hungry for more— and thirsty for a closer, more vibrant, more trusting, more empowered, and more fulfilling relationship with God.

You see, God wants to heal you. Fill you. Embrace you. Share with you. Encourage you. Challenge you. God wants you to live fully, joyfully, enthusiastically as a child of heaven and to live out that fullness by loving and serving others. God wants all that for you and more. Experiencing it starts with a sensitive, listening heart, a willing spirit, an active mind. Jesus asks you, *"Are your ears awake? Listen. Listen to the Wind Words, the Spirit blowing through the churches" (Revelation 2:29, The Messsage).*

Author's Note: I once heard the Rev. Gray Temple, Jr.—my first rector and a beloved mentor—use the phrase "a generous beckoning" in a sermon at St. Patrick's Episcopal Church in Dunwoody, Georgia. Obviously, it stuck with me over the years since. I am grateful for the many ways Gray helped to form my faith and ministry.

I

THE
CREATIVE SOURCE
AND YOU

*God the Father's Invitations to You
from the Old Testament*

God Beckons You
to Trust

1. Making Life Happen

> God blessed them, and said to them, "Be
> fruitful and multiply, and fill the earth and
> subdue it; and have dominion over the fish of
> the sea and over the birds of the air and over
> every living thing that moves upon the earth."
> —GENESIS 1:28

God trusts you.

Let that powerful notion sink into your heart. The Bible says
human beings were created "in the image of God" (Genesis
1:27). And that nature is marked by creativity, productivity,
choice, and authority.

Not only did God create us with the divine image, but also God blessed us. God spoke powerful words of invitation and command over the very first humans, our forebears. And God speaks the same words to you.

In *The Message*, verse 28 reads, "Prosper! Reproduce! Fill Earth! Take charge!"

God says, "Go for it!" Make life happen. Reproduce what's good and holy and true in you, and spread it around to others. Fill the planet with righteousness and justice and holy truth. Exercise fruitful, faithful, servant-like dominion.

"Take charge!"

In creating us as human beings, God has gifted us with all the wisdom and resources and strength we need to fulfill this calling. And we have the Holy Spirit dwelling within us to empower and guide us.

How can we open ourselves up to this truth? How can we accept God's gracious invitation to "take charge"?

When I became the head of a well-known ecumenical media ministry that's now more than 75 years old, I must admit the prospects were energizing. The foundation of the organization had been well set and was solid. The sky was the limit.

During the first several months, I was a tornado of energy, making overdue improvements to our weekly radio program, pursuing new broadcast outlets, restoring neglected relationships with other organizations, revamping our website, and cultivating new donors.

It was energizing because I knew I had to trust and depend on God completely. That's because I didn't have a clue as to what I was doing. I had a wide range of experience that informed me and plenty of smart people to support me. But I was determined to launch out, go all in, approach problems with fresh creativity, believe in this calling, and let myself be invigorated by the potential of this ministry.

After a few years on the job, I started doing the same right, good things in my own strength. I began to function on autopilot, focusing on what I had accomplished. My dependency on God began to slip ever so slightly. My strength ebbed away into exhaustion; my enthusiasm dwindled into negativity. When harder times came for the organization, I had few resources to draw on.

Feel familiar? Is that where you are too? I have been there many times. And I will no doubt return there again. For me, in the more than twenty years since that early time, I have learned—hopefully more times than not—how to keep trusting God and pushing the limits so that the ministry can continue to thrive despite the complex roller coaster of our times.

✤ When you find yourself in that place, remember: "God blessed them." And God blesses you.

✤ God blesses you when you lift your eyes to heaven and recognize this invitation to be productive and proactive. When you renew your trust in the God who urges and cheers you on. When you drink deep from the bottomless pool of divine wisdom and strength. When you let go of your own fears and fetters. When you rely on all who have been called along with you.

✤ And when God blesses you, then you are set free to prosper.

It won't happen if you don't trust God with everything you are and with everything you have.

And it won't happen if you don't trust that you were created to be part of this amazing responsibility to make life happen.

God trusts you.

God, I am overwhelmed by the responsibility you place on me, the trust you have in me to serve you in creative and meaningful ways. I accept your challenge. Give me the trust, wisdom, and vision I need to make it happen. For your glory. Amen.

2. Climbing Higher

> Come up to me on the mountain, and wait
> there; and I will give you the tablets of stone,
> with the law and the commandment, which I
> have written for their instruction.
> —EXODUS 24:12

God invites Moses to "come up to me...and wait."

Doesn't that sound familiar?

Doesn't our life sometimes feel as though we are constantly climbing higher and higher, trying to negotiate the crumbling rock around us in order to reach the plateau where God and perfection and security and serenity can be authentically experienced and fully enjoyed? And doesn't it seem like we must constantly wait for all that without ever really reaching it?

We just keep climbing and waiting. And our trust in God fades.

Ernest Shackleton and his crew must have known what that felt like. They sailed for the South Pole in their ship, the Endurance, in August 1914. The crew of twenty-seven planned to make history as the first people (the first white men, at any rate) to cross Antarctica.

But the harsh realities of the Antarctic soon threatened not only the mission but also their very lives. Early on, the Endurance became trapped in the ice, where it remained stuck for ten months before the ice crushed the wooden vessel. The men lived on the ice floe for the next five months, then left in lifeboats.

They made it to Elephant Island. They found themselves alone on the rocky, icy island, desperate for help. Shackleton took five men in a lifeboat in a last-ditch attempt at survival. While the remaining crewmen waited, this paltry crew hoped to make it to South Georgia Island, a base for whaling operations. It was eight hundred miles away.

Miraculously, they made it—but they landed on the side of the island *opposite* the inhabited areas.

There's a heart-stopping scene in a motion picture account of their true story in which the crew members hike across the desolate island. Their supplies, food, and wits exhausted, they believe that if they can climb over the mountain and reach the whalers' supply outpost, they will be well on their way home. The climb is treacherous and challenging; slowly they inch their way up the rough, icy, windswept mountain.

The summit finally looms into view—they are nearly there. But when they finally reach the top and look beyond, they see, stretching into apparent infinity, a whole range of similarly threatening mountains—twenty-six miles of mountains, in fact—that had to be crossed if they were to survive.

Doesn't that just feel like life?

We spend difficult years in school pursuing our life dreams— only to find that the reality of the world affords little in the way of perfection when it comes to job or career.

We work hard at making our relationships and our family life as positive and authentic as we can—and yet the struggles and conflicts only seem to deepen.

We plan and fret and work hard to make ends meet—and a major unexpected expense blindsides us.

We study, we pray, we sacrifice in trying to grow closer to God, to build our faith—and only feel a growing distance that seems impossible to breach.

"Come up to me...and wait."

What was God thinking? What kind of invitation is that?

It's the kind of invitation that builds solid, unshakable, mature faith. It is the kind of good news that develops trust in the God who will meet us there, who will climb with us and wait with us and ultimately give us all the provisions we need.

Shackleton and his five crewmembers succeeded in their incredible mountainous trek. And with the boats sent to rescue those left on Elephant Island, his entire crew—all 27 of them—survived their two-year ordeal. They navigated impossible odds and got through. They made it home.

Trusting in God's help and direction, you can too.

God, when I have climbed through life expecting something glorious, the last thing I want to do is wait. Give me patience. Build my trust. For I know that the result will be something I will cherish for the rest of my life. Amen.

3. The Utter Truth

So acknowledge today and take to heart
that the LORD is God in heaven above and
on the earth beneath; there is no other.
—DEUTERONOMY 4:39

∽◈∾

Moses bears witness to Israel that there is a God. The only God there is. A God who, by the way, is not you.

When I am stewing in fear or stress or frustration about something going on in my life or in the life of someone I love, I have to ask myself: am I trusting in God? Am I behaving in a way that shows my belief in God in heaven and on earth, the God who is almighty, omnipotent, and working in love and power and grace in the world?

When I am pursuing behaviors or activities that I know are not in God's best interests for me, ones that may be unhealthy physically or emotionally or spiritually, I have to ask myself: am I acknowledging that the omniscient God is present with me? Am I taking to heart the knowledge that I am God's, completely?

When I check the news headlines with trepidation and anxiety, concerned about the turmoil and hunger and hatred around the world, I have to ask myself: am I aware that God is the only God there is? Do I really trust this omnipresent God?

When I grieve over the serious illness of someone I love dearly or deal with their death, I have to ask myself: do I believe in my heart of hearts that the all-loving God is here with me, that the person who died is with God forever, and that, yes, God is in control?

Life is filled with falsehood and doubt. When you get down to it, how many people can you really, truly count on, no matter what? How many truths do you really know beyond all uncertainty?

There is one truth on which you can stand, a truth you would do well to accept fully. No matter where you are in life or what you're dealing with, this is the truth that should permeate your experience: *"The Lord is God in heaven above and on the earth beneath; there is no other."*

This is where you start.

This is what you trust, what you stake your life on.

This is the substance of your faith.

This is what you know as unshakable, unyielding, absolute reality in a world seemingly devoid of absolutes: the God you know, the God who knows you, is the God who lovingly rules the universe. It's this God, or nothing.

Take that to heart right now.

❦

God, I believe in you. I trust you. I rest in you. At least I say I do. Help me to really mean it. And know it. And take it to heart. Amen.

4. Pay Attention

Hear, O Israel: The LORD is our God, the LORD
alone. You shall love the LORD your God with
all your heart, and with all your soul, and with
all your might. —DEUTERONOMY 6:4-5

❦

This familiar invitation of God through Moses is a special verse
for Jewish people, who call it the *Shema* for the Hebrew word
for hear. Many repeat it daily to remind them of the heart and
soul of their faith.

"Hear, O Israel"—*listen carefully.* The Hebrew word for hear
coaxes us to pay attention, to listen diligently. It's not like
hearing music playing in the background. It's an intentional,
focused listening with everything we have and are, every fiber
of our being, to the voice of God.

We hear in this way because this God matters. This God
is "the Lord alone." This God is our God. This is the God
we trust.

I usually regard as extremely suspect accounts of people who
say they hear the voice of God speaking directly to them. But
I vividly remember a time many years ago when I heard God

speak to me. It wasn't an audible voice, but I clearly heard the words spoken in love to my distressed mind.

At the time, I was upset about the downward trend of a close friendship. My friend and I had spent lots of time together in church and at play—praying together, hiking together, eating lunch together, just being together. But we had entered a serious rough spot in our friendship as other relationships and responsibilities claimed more and more of his time. I was becoming too dependent, and he was reacting to my neediness, perhaps unconsciously, by putting even more distance between us.

As the relationship deteriorated, my fears increased. I worried I would lose this meaningful friendship completely because of the choices he had made—and I was blind to the choices I'd made. My anxiety grew over the very real possibility that the rich relationship we had enjoyed for several years was coming to an end, perhaps forever. And this fear caused me to become increasingly needy with him, with the result that I wasn't much fun to be around, so he only avoided me more—which further fed my fear.

It was a frustrating cycle of pain, and it consumed far too much of my attention and energy.

One morning, in self-absorbed misery, I cried out to God, begging for a change in my friend's attitude so we could go back to the way things were. After all, wasn't I a terrific person?

Why didn't my friend appreciate me as he should? I was in a total wad of self-centered, clueless despair.

That I could hear God in the midst of that self-pity is a miracle in itself. But the words came with crystal clarity into my mind, like clean, fresh rainfall on dry, parched earth: *Let go of the fear, and the love will remain.*

When I heard those words, I nearly jumped out of my easy chair with the recognition that God was speaking to me, reassuring me, instructing me lovingly and giving me hope. It seemed clear to me me: if only I could be bold enough to let go of my fear in the relationship, I would discover that our love and friendship would remain.

I could feel myself relax. And trust. My anxiety dissolved into peace.

Over time, I sensed a new balance in this friendship. I began to apply this principle of fearless trust to other relationships in my life.

Perhaps ironically, my friend and his wife and new family moved away a year or so later. I'm rather surprised to admit that these days we only connect once a year or so.

As I look back, I realize the words I heard may not have been meant only for that relationship but for all my life. My relationships fell back into balance over time, and I dealt with some vitally important issues of my life with trusted mentors and counselors. Today, I am more content and fulfilled than ever.

Let go of the fear, and the love will remain. That reality has emboldened me to live more fully, to risk loving, to work diligently at being who I truly am as God made me.

Is God trying to tell you something in the midst of your fear or doubt or sadness? Listen. What you hear could change your life.

And the first thing we hear from God through Moses in this passage is a reminder to keep first things first: "You shall love the Lord your God with all your heart, and with all your soul, and with all your might."

Love God wholly, with everything we are. When we hear and obey this command, when we learn to lean on God with everything we have within us, when we pay attention and accept this invitation to a full-bodied, full-spirited, full-hearted, full-minded love of our God, there's no telling what we will be able to hear God saying to us.

Pay attention.

God, open my ears and my heart to the whisper of your Spirit. Help me to pay attention to the way you work in my life. Help me to love you with all I have. Because you are the one and only. Amen.

God Beckons You to Responsibility

5. A Living Responsibility

> Have dominion over the fish of the sea and over
> the birds of the air and over every living thing
> that moves upon the earth. —GENESIS 1:28B

God invites you to take full responsibility for all the other
life on this planet—for "every living thing that moves upon
the earth."

Think of the ramifications. If you took responsibility for God's
full panoply of creation, what would that look like?

Would you take a greater interest in the environment? Would
you be involved in the policies of your government and various
corporations regarding preserving it and cleaning it up?

Would you be concerned about the treatment of animals raised to satisfy your physical needs? Or about the survival of species threatened by human invasion?

Would you take more opportunities to enjoy the great outdoors responsibly? To see it, experience, and spend time surrounded by natural beauty?

Seriously, what would you do if you took this invitation to heart?

As a young man (and perhaps again one of these days) one of my most favorite activities was camping. When my kids were young, I would try to get them into the outdoors at least once or twice a year to experience nature and enjoy the rhythms of life outdoors. Or, I would go camping with friends for a little camaraderie. It always felt good and restorative and holy to spend time outside.

In recent years my spouse, Dan, and I enjoyed a beat-up little cabin outside of Cashiers, North Carolina, on Lake Glenville. We bought it when it was in the midst of a much-needed renovation—which had not gotten very far. Slowly, over ten years, much work was done, though much remained. Even so, nothing in the world compared to sitting on that rickety porch and gazing out at the trees and the mountains and a little slice of Lake Glenville.

Experiencing the seasons there was a joy—from lush summer greenery to the wildly colorful spectacle of autumn, then from the traceries of the empty tree limbs and branches opening new unseen vistas to the fresh green rising in spring. The mountain laurel and rhododendrons and day lilies and blazing dahlias added fragrance and color as they danced in the breeze.

During rejuvenating but too-rare weekends, we spent wonderful moments together walking around the lake neighborhoods and horse meadow, staring at the crystal stars, driving country roads and gasping at the verdant vistas before us, or simply sitting and gazing at the peaceful lake from that rickety porch.

Alas, we finally sold our little cabin. But I learned again that being outside in God's creation invigorates the senses and helps us reset our overly digitized souls. It enables us to be in touch with the Creator, so we can appreciate not only the creation but also the One who so skillfully put it together for our use and enjoyment.

But as much as God delights in our enjoyment of nature, we need to remind ourselves that we do not own this planet, our island home. It belongs to its Creator. We are simply caretakers, tenants, stewards who are responsible for its upkeep. Yes, *responsible.*

Life on this planet is beautiful and rich and teeming. God beckons to you, welcoming you into this wondrous world, urging you to experience it. Enjoy it—and take responsibility to care for it.

God, thank you for the gift of this planet. Help me accept my share of the responsibility for caring for it. As I enjoy the riches of creation, keep me mindful of the need to keep it clean and healthy and thriving. Amen.

6. *Following the Crowd*

> You shall not follow a majority in wrongdoing;
> when you bear witness in a lawsuit, you shall
> not side with the majority so as to pervert
> justice. —EXODUS 23:2

⊂◉⊃

God invites us to take responsibility. To stand up for what's right, even if we're standing there all alone.

This means not necessarily going along with the crowd or saying or doing things for the approval of those around you.

You may think peer pressure is something only young people face. But ask yourself whether you have ever done something because your friends or coworkers were doing it—even though you felt uncomfortable about it? If you're like me, the answer is yes. We want to be liked or feel like part of the gang. Maybe we are still seeking the approval of a parent (even one who is no longer alive).

Why is it so hard to do what's right in a world where it seems anything goes?

It all boils down to acceptance. We want to be accepted and loved and appreciated and enjoyed by those around us. And we will do whatever it takes to ensure they do.

So, when others get caught up in mischief—or worse—we go right along. We do or say what we think everyone else wants us to do or say, just so they'll continue to approve of us. And before we realize it, we've crossed a line, hurting ourselves or others as the result of our selfish fears.

God's word to us through Moses is simple: Don't follow the crowd in doing something harmful or hurtful. It's certainly a ready piece of advice parents give their children over the years—and advice children often ignore or reject. And to be honest: so did we when we were young—and probably still do from time to time.

An "everybody does it" attitude infects all of us. When we drive, we ignore speed limits or stop signs. When we do our taxes, we embellish our deductions. When we have a free evening, we go out with the gang instead of spending some much needed time with a neglected spouse or children. When we write our resumes and complete job applications, we make sure we look as good as possible—or even better.

What's the harm? Everybody does it.

But God beckons us to responsibility, to moral strength.

God urges us to build righteous boundaries, knowing how far we should go to protect ourselves and others.

God promises us the spiritual strength to stand strong in the face of temptation and to keep firm to those boundaries of behavior. If we adopt an "everybody does it" attitude with the little things, what's to keep it from infecting us at deeper levels?

Standing up for what's right may not please some people, but perhaps we shouldn't be trying to please them anyway. Yet displaying moral responsibility will please God, whose acceptance of us is really all that matters.

I may be coming across as a goody-two-shoes here. But I hope you will like me anyway.

⚬⚬⚬

God, give me the courage to take responsibility and do what's right. Give me strength to make choices that honor you and your will for me, no matter what anyone else does or what others may think of me. I am so grateful that I don't have to do anything to prove you love me because I know you accept me as I am. Amen.

7. Judging Justly

> You shall not render an unjust judgment;
> you shall not be partial to the poor or defer
> to the great: with justice you shall judge your
> neighbor. —LEVITICUS 19:15

⚬

Not long ago, I ran into an acquaintance who was stewing in self-righteous anger. His college-age son had been caught on campus doing something he wasn't supposed to be doing— "harmless frat fun," the father explained—and was hauled before the student judicial board.

The college, of course, had distributed to every student a rather thorough and explicit handbook, a detailed code of conduct with carefully worded consequences for specific infractions. And when that code was violated, the appropriate punishment was meted out, much to the chagrin of the student—and his father.

My acquaintance—an alumnus of the same college who had become rather successful in the business world—never came out and specifically said the words, "Don't they know who I am?" But I know that was exactly the question reverberating in his head. It was spilling out all over the place, in fact. You could almost see him figuring up in his mind exactly how much his next alumni contribution to the school would not be.

But the board of student judges was simply following the clear rules, doing what was right and fair, regardless of the identity (or legacy) of the perpetrator.

Unfortunately, judicial proceedings are not always so just. Occasionally, the poor are given a pass because they're disadvantaged, but more often, they are treated even more harshly...because they're disadvantaged. The same is true with the rich: they sometimes seem to get away with murder, though occasionally, judges will make a harsh example of them.

God encourages us through Moses not to pervert justice but to be responsible to do what's right—no matter who is involved. That sounds so simple, but it can be difficult to fulfill.

From cover to cover, the Bible is clear that the poor and needy are always close to God's heart. But that's no reason to ignore their wrongdoing or excuse sin. A law broken by a poor person is still a broken law. But perhaps we ought to dig deeper into the causes *behind* the broken law. What drove the perpetrator to this point? What can be done to improve the situation?

On the other hand, just because someone is wealthy, powerful, or important should not mean they have a perpetual "get out of jail free" pass. They too are responsible for their own actions. Just look at business news reports, and you'll likely see one prominent person after another, in business, politics, sports, or entertainment, being hauled before a judge or otherwise in serious trouble.

The point is, no matter who commits wrong, it's still wrong. Economic or corporate or political status should have no influence on the process of justice. And while we may not be involved in the legal system, we are still judges of our fellow humans. We encounter and pass judgment on numerous folks every day.

When someone cuts us off in traffic, we try, sentence, and condemn them in a flash. When someone rushes to the last open seat on the train before we do, we curse them silently— whatever happened to chivalry? When someone gets caught embezzling from their company or cheating on their spouse, we shake our heads with a superior air.

All those actions may be wrong. But we also must ask ourselves about whether we judge more harshly if the person is of a different race. What if the person is covered with tattoos and piercings, driving a car that costs ten times what you paid for yours, wearing a turban or hijab, or donning a particular political candidate's cap?

Is your self-righteous reaction just a bit more superior?

The justice of God, the justice God seeks, is pure and righteous and perfect. Don't show favoritism in either direction, rich or poor. Take responsibility to do what is right. Judge justly.

You do that by looking at each person as a person, each act as an act. And you can do that only in God's wisdom and strength.

❧

God, it's so easy to judge people based on externals. But you look upon the heart. Give me a heart of compassionate justice, one that reflects your righteousness. And help me not to judge others but to leave that in your capable hands. Amen.

8. Strangers and Aliens

> When an alien resides with you in your land,
> you shall not oppress the alien. The alien who
> resides with you shall be to you as the citizen
> among you; you shall love the alien as yourself,
> for you were aliens in the land of Egypt: I am
> the LORD your God. —LEVITICUS 19:33-34

⤫

Wilfred was the first Black man I can remember relating to or, to be honest, even knowing. He was tall, slim, with skin the shade of a moonless, dusty midnight sky and blazing white teeth. I had trouble understanding him; his accent, though musical, was thick and strange to my four-year-old ears. One of his arms was malformed or had been injured. But he smiled a lot. He seemed to be a merry man.

Wilfred was an exchange student studying medicine at the university in the city where my father was a pastor at the time. For a year or so in the late 1950s, Wilfred lived in the garage apartment behind my family's parsonage on Grand Avenue in Morgantown, West Virginia.

I can still see clearly the shiny new Ford Edsel my father parked in front of the two-story garage. I peddled my black and white metal police car around and around it—the driveway was pretty much the only level surface on our steeply inclined block. After his classes, Wilfred would come home and greet me warmly as he walked up the wooden staircase to his humble apartment. In my memory, he is always wearing a dark suit and a thin necktie over a bright white dress shirt.

My folks would invite him to join us for supper on occasion, especially on Sundays, and as we broke bread together, he would tell our family amazing stories about growing up in Liberia, a land that seemed strange and distant to me. After completing medical school, he intended to return home and serve his people as a doctor.

Wilfred was certainly different from all the other people around me at the time. My very young mind could hardly understand how it must have felt for him to live as a Black man, a foreigner, an alien in 1950s America just at the brink of the Civil Rights movement and its often-violent conflicts with the status quo.

All I knew was that he was friendly. And he smiled a lot.

Looking back, I hope he felt the same about us.

North America has changed dramatically in the past six or seven decades. We have continued to experience an influx of immigrants from all over the world, not only Africa, but also Mexico and Central and South America, Asia, the Middle East, Europe. In Atlanta, areas of town that were formerly home to white suburbanites have become a colorful and diverse mixture of Latino/Hispanic and Asian culture.

Sometimes, frankly, this makes me uncomfortable. It can feel like outsiders are encroaching on my turf.

Then I read this verse. And I think of what Wilfred must have experienced. And I open my ears and my heart to God's generous beckoning to take responsibility, to "love them as yourself."

After all, we're all strangers and aliens here. We're just passing through. And God deeply desires that we enjoy the journey with one another.

⚮

God, help me to be responsible to see others, no matter who they are or where they're from, as brothers or sisters or siblings. Help me love them like one of my own. After all, that's who they are. Amen.

9. Stand Up

> The Lord said to Joshua, "Stand up! Why have
> you fallen upon your face?" —Joshua 7:10

❧

Suddenly, everything was falling apart.

One sinful act by one person, Achan, threatened to undo all
the progress Israel had made under Joshua in the land God was
giving them. After Israel miraculously defeated Jericho, Achan
pilfered some valuable contraband from the city—forbidden
booty most likely related to idolatrous worship. And that
sinful act led to the shattering consequence of utter defeat by
the forces of Ai.

The Israelites had confidently spied out the land and the
resulting plan of attack seemed sound. There was only one
problem: it didn't work.

The soldiers of Ai swarmed against the Israelites and struck
them down. And Israel experienced defeat for the first time in
their seemingly unstoppable quest for the Promised Land.

Joshua was shocked and devastated by the setback. He fell face
to the ground before the ark of the Lord, weeping desperately
before God for hours. Here's how *The Message* puts it:

Oh, oh, oh…Master, GOD. Why did you insist on
bringing this people across the Jordan? To make us
victims of the Amorites? To wipe us out? Why didn't
we just settle down on the east side of the Jordan? Oh,
Master, what can I say after this, after Israel has been
run off by its enemies? When the Canaanites and all
the others living here get wind of this, they'll gang
up on us and make short work of us—and then how
will you keep up *your* reputation? (Joshua 7:7-9, *The
Message*).

I can see myself right there, feeling devastated and abandoned
like Joshua. And that's so typical, isn't it? One surprise attack,
one single reversal, and we want to give up. We feel like
throwing the whole bathtub out the window, baby, water, and
all. We writhe in self-absorbed agony, questioning God.

How could God treat us so? What happened to all those loving
promises? Doesn't God realize what this will mean to us? How
could God be so foolish? Doesn't God understand how bad
this makes us—and God!—look to the rest of the world?

God finally silenced Joshua's distress, saying, "Stand up." Stop
whining and groveling. Be strong in the face of this setback.
Take responsibility for what has happened. Know that God is
with you, but there are some things you must deal with.

Israel had sinned. Yes, just one Israelite, Achan, had actually
broken God's law. But they were one people, one family.

And the wrongful act of one infected all: "They've broken
the covenant I commanded them; they've taken forbidden
plunder—stolen and then covered up the theft, squirreling it
away with their own stuff" (Joshua 7:11, *The Message*).

You see, a covenant works both ways. God's promises are
fulfilled in obedient hearts.

Thankfully, self-defeated lives can be made new again. God
instructed Joshua: "So get started. Purify the people. Tell them:
Get ready for tomorrow by purifying yourselves" (Joshua 7:13,
The Message).

Certainly, not all setbacks in life are the consequence of bad
choices or wrong actions. But those things have consequences.
When you find yourself suffering over a loss or a setback
caused by wrongdoing, when you find yourself questioning
God's sanity and doubting God's loving promises as Joshua
did, listen to the divine invitation to stand up. Take
responsibility. Get clean if you need to. Make things right if
necessary.

And then get back to it.

God, help me to see your hand behind the circumstances of my life. If I need to deal with sin and separation from you, help me to do that. If I need to stand up and move on, then give me the strength to do that. Amen.

God Beckons You
to Your Life Purpose

10. Leaving Home

> Now the LORD said to Abram, "Go from your
> country and your kindred and your father's
> house to the land that I will show you."
> —GENESIS 12:1

⬥

There comes a time we all must leave home, comfort,
familiarity, and security and to step out into an unknown
land—the future God has for us. Our life purpose.

For me, it all started on Memorial Day weekend in 1976.
The two-hour drive from my parents' home in Charleston
to Richwood, West Virginia, was sheer delight. The weather

was sunny, the temperature warm, and I was free. I had just graduated from college, and my first job awaited me.

I was heading for the Tidewater area of Virginia to spend the holiday on the James River with my folks—one last bit of fun before entering the workaday world as an adult. On my way, I would side-trip through Richwood to touch base before being added to the payroll of *The West Virginia Hillbilly,* a weekly newspaper edited and published by one of the state's most beloved eccentrics, Jim Comstock.

The *Hillbilly* sought to overturn the eponymous stereotype by focusing on the arts, literature, history, and politics of the state, past and present. It had quite a reputation in its time as well for the cynical wit and wisdom shared on the back-page essays offered under the heading, "The Comstock Load." My grandparents had subscribed for years and often shared copies with my folks, which I devoured as a kid. Now I was actually going to work for this legend. But first, I made a preview visit on the way to the rendezvous with my family.

I had taken the scenic route along the mountainous and winding State Route 60. The next leg from Summersville to Richwood on Route 39 was breathtaking, with rambunctious curves and bucolic views that tested the steering of my "new" used Ford. Before long, I was driving through the little village of Fenwick, crossing a bridge and climbing a hill. As I crested the top, the beautiful small town of Richwood spread out before me, filling the Cherry River Valley, surrounded by lush, wooded hills. It was a postcard vision. Even so, my heart was filled with nervous anticipation.

I didn't have a clue as to what I would be doing on the job, how much I would be paid for it, or even where I would live. Since I would start in just a few days, I hoped it would all get worked out. Perhaps this day, for a change, I would get some concrete answers from my soon-to-be-boss.

I found the rickety, white frame Palotta Building smack in the middle of town, right next to a bustling Union 76 gas station at the only intersection in town with a traffic light. At the time, this modest, ancient structure was the *Hillbilly* World Headquarters. On the bottom right half of the building was the Hillbilly Bookstore, crammed with books by, for, and about West Virginians, some of them published by Comstock himself. In the bottom left half was an office housing Jim's assistant, Dot, and the work areas for the newspaper.

Upstairs was a suite of offices, most of them filled completely, floor to ceiling, with books and papers. Overlooking Main Street and stretching across the entire front of the building was Jim's ephemera-strewn office. Behind it were rooms used primarily for storage. Hallways and rooms seemed to have been added on to the back of the Palotta Building without much thought of a plan.

I spent a half-hour getting the nickel tour of the building and chatting with Jim about getting started after the Memorial

Day holiday. He graciously offered to let me live in an apartment. Right on the premises.

He took me upstairs to show it to me. "This…will be your room," he announced proudly. "You can live here," he added, as though trying to convince me he was telling the truth.

Truth is, I was stunned. I looked at this little room tucked back behind his office. It was filled literally from floor to ceiling with books, boxes, papers, and assorted odds and ends. It did have a window, but the view was just the brick wall of the building next door. The space between the buildings, about a yard wide, had been covered and used for, you guessed it, more storage.

Just behind this ten-by-twelve-foot room was a bathroom. I could tell because I noticed the claw feet of an old bathtub underneath a piled mound of ephemera. It too was filled with a great variety of interesting things, some of which apparently had been alive at one time.

I smiled weakly. I'm sure I was pale. Sensing my chagrin, Comstock quickly assured me, "I'll get some handymen to clean this out and paint it and get a couch in here for you to sleep on. It'll be ready by the time you get back on Monday."

Okay. Sure. This was Thursday.

Many thoughts tumbled through my head, but I figured, hey, I was young and flexible. Resilient! Right?

I left shortly thereafter, wondering what in the world I was getting myself into. Was Comstock as harebrained as I was gathering? Did he really know what he was asking of me— forcing me to live in a tiny room surrounded by piles of old stuff?

I tried to forget my doubts that weekend and managed to enjoy the time with my family in Virginia. But my heart was full of concern on the drive back that next Monday. I arrived in late afternoon.

And sure enough, that little room had been transformed. It was clean, painted, furnished…and home. I can't imagine the work that had been required just to haul the materials somewhere else. I was impressed.

That room would be my home for nearly a year. And there was only one problem with it. It was right next door to Jim's office. He came in every morning about six o'clock. And turned on the TV. Loud. And started to work on his manual typewriter, which sounded like a machine gun.

This generally woke me up. So, I'd take a bath in that classy old cleaned-out tub, get dressed, and head across the street to a family-owned restaurant for breakfast. Then I'd report to work by about seven.

I worked for Jim Comstock for three years and two months. It was an awesome experience, especially if one enjoyed living on the edge. When I woke up every morning, I would have no idea where I might end up that night.

First thing every day, I'd enter that front office—the room filled with intriguing piles of ancient books, yesterday's mail, printouts to proofread, unfinished articles, and piles of back issues—and report for duty.

"Pete!" he'd bark in an energetic, high-pitched voice, "Here's what I want you to do today."

And I'd be off on another adventure. Perhaps it was to cover a coal miners' march in Washington, D.C., or oversee the printing of a special 200-page newspaper issue celebrating the nation's Bicentennial. Sell ad space to some very dubious businessmen or take Jim's place as grand marshal in a small-town parade. Give a speech at a Pearl Buck Birthplace Chautauqua or typeset some headlines and paste up some pages. Cover the state legislature session or interview the just-elected governor, Jay Rockefeller. Investigate old railroad ghost towns or simply chauffeur Jim to a speaking engagement while he wrote his lively editorial essays on a yellow legal pad.[3]

What if I hadn't taken that terrifying step? What if I hadn't listened to God's inward call? I would have lost a lifetime of wonderful memories packed into those three-plus years. And, knowing that it's all part of my journey now, I may never have ended up where God has blessed me so richly.

Fast-forward 25 years from that day in 1976, where my life path led me to a Middle Eastern restaurant in Atlanta and lunch with the Rev. Canon Louis "Skip" Schueddig, executive director of the Episcopal Media Center.

Not too long before this lunch I had met with my rector, Gray Temple Jr., asking him for advice on how to discern God's calling for me at this point in my life. After more than a decade of working at an advertising agency, I was yearning to serve God in a more responsible position, in a ministry where I could feel useful and at home. Among other helpful pieces of advice, Gray had suggested that Skip and I meet and explore some options.

Over the process of several monthly lunch meetings, Skip and I formed a friendship that, thanks to his encouragement, ultimately became a close working relationship at the *Day 1* and Episcopal Media Center ministry, where I've spent the last 22 years answering God's call and exercising my ministry.

Oh, I'm certainly no Abram. But I do hope to be a willing child of God, sensitive to divine coaxing, open to God's calling for me—no matter how overwhelming, strange, and faraway it might appear.

How about you?

And what's God calling us to next?

God, make me sensitive to your calling on my life, responsive to your beckoning to me moment by moment. Like Abram, I want to heed the call without hesitation, because my trust in you is solid and ever growing. Amen.

11. In Abram's Sandals

> After these things the word of the LORD came
> to Abram in a vision, "Do not be afraid,
> Abram, I am your shield; your reward shall be
> very great." —GENESIS 15:1

⚜

Life is way too busy, isn't it? Each day seems full of stress, job responsibilities, financial pressures, and family static mixed in with just enough fulfillment, hope, and rest to taunt us. All of it can wear us down, empty us of hopeful energy, and fill us with the fear that it's only going to get worse.

And then we read a verse like this. "After these things," it begins. And we flip back over the previous chapters of Genesis to see what all "these things" might include.

Let's see: there's a call to abandon the status quo and launch out into the unknown at the word of a God few people really know much about (Genesis 12:1).

There's a huge responsibility placed on the shoulders of an aging man to establish a vast nation (12:2-3).

There's a difficult reconnaissance of the land with a selfish nephew, dealing with often-unsavory characters already living in this land that has supposedly been given him by God (12:4—13:18).

There's a death-defying rescue of that nephew from a consortium of warring kings involving armed battle with resulting success (14).

Whew. Abram managed to get through all that and more in order to answer the call of God on his life. And it had to have raised some negative feelings in his soul.

Abram had been a wealthy, successful, yet simple man wedged deeply in the status quo when God called him to step out and do something astonishingly dramatic... with the ultimate promise of a magnificent nation and eternal glory.

And now God reassures Abram in the midst of the apparent chaos of the aftermath of his decision to step out in obedience.

Are you doing what God has called you to do? Stepping out boldly, unhesitatingly, full of trust and confidence into God's life purpose for you? If so, God's inviting words to Abram are also God's words for you: "Do not be afraid...I am your shield; your reward shall be very great."

If you still find yourself ensconced comfortably in Ur, what do you need to do, where do you need to go, so that you can know God's fearless protection while you answer God's call on your life?

❦

God, it's clear that the vast responsibility and the unexpected incidents in his life would have overwhelmed Abram if he hadn't trusted you with his whole heart. I admire the results of his obedience. And I yearn for that same level of faith. Help me to step out without fear in the sure knowledge that you are my shield, too. Amen.

12. Be Strong and Courageous

> Only be strong and very courageous, being
> careful to act in accordance with all the law
> that my servant Moses commanded you; do not
> turn from it to the right hand or to the left, so
> that you may be successful wherever you go.
> —JOSHUA 1:7

⟨∾⟩

Can you imagine being in Joshua's sandals? How do you follow an act like Moses?

Moses had accomplished the impossible-made-inevitable: he had led the large, boisterous, doubting, needy nation of Israel out of their Egyptian captivity and through the punishing wilderness for 40 difficult years.

Now this nation of hundreds of thousands of people stood, without their familiar leader, on the brink of a whole new life. At last, the Promised Land lay before them.

God gave Joshua his marching orders: "Be strong and courageous; for you shall put this people in possession of the land that I swore to their ancestors to give them" (Joshua 1:6).

But it certainly wasn't going to be a walk in the park to cross the Jordan River and enter the already occupied land.

God placed an immense weight of responsibility on Joshua's shoulders. Fulfilling his life purpose required incredible organizational skills. Limitless trust in God. And the inner resources to handle the incomprehensible needs of so many people.

How must he have felt? I can't imagine.

But God didn't give Joshua an impossible goal without also providing the resources, the encouragement, and the wisdom necessary to fulfill it.

God's word to Joshua was simple and clear: "Be strong and courageous." Give it everything you've got—go for it with your whole heart, soul, mind, and strength—not only to enter and subdue the land but also to trust fully, to obey every part of God's word, which Moses had so carefully taught.

That's step one: trusting God. If that step isn't taken first, if that isn't the top priority of any effort, then none of the other steps needed to enter and dwell within the Promised Land would lead to success.

I am certainly no Joshua, but I think I've sensed a minuscule bit of the fear and uncertainty he must have felt. I'm sure you can identify with him as well. When I was ordained as a priest after several years in a discernment process and some additional Episcopal studies courses, I found myself standing with my toes in the water on the other side of the Jordan, looking across to the immensity of the calling ahead of me.

Sure, I had some experience in most aspects of the work of the church, but I had never been the responsible one, the one on whose desk the buck stopped. I had always been the assistant to the leader or a layperson helping out. A Joshua to a Moses.

Now this particular mantle had fallen on me. I could easily have run backward in terror into the hills. Or I could give it everything I had, heart and soul. My mantra during this life-changing time was, "All In." I would be as obedient to God's calling as I possibly could, with all the resources and strength God's Spirit could provide. And then I could trust God to lead me.

A funny thing happens when you give your life goal everything you've got. Regardless of your calling, when you devote yourself heart and soul, you find yourself carried along by the lively and life-giving Spirit of God into new worlds. You discover resources and abilities within that you never knew you possessed. You experience a creative energy you've never tapped into before.

There's no question you will also be exhausted, stymied, discouraged, and frustrated beyond anything you've ever known, as I certainly have been. But that's simply part of the process. That's what finding yourself in the rushing movement of God's will is all about.

And yet, the guaranteed result of pure, wholehearted, courageous, surrendered obedience is that you will get to where you're going. And you will relish the journey. Because you are giving it all you've got. You are living your life fully.

You are all in.

❧

God, you've set a calling before me. I want to give it everything I've got, heart and soul and mind and strength. Ease my fears and doubts by building my faith in you. Amen.

God Beckons You to Holiness

13. Holy Ground

> God said, "Come no closer! Remove the sandals from your feet, for the place on which you are standing is holy ground." —Exodus 3:5

A brother in the faith and I walked the hilly wooded path to a rock outcropping, an expanse of gray granite that topped a hill bordering Camp Mikell, the camp and conference center for the Episcopal Diocese of Atlanta outside Toccoa in Northeast Georgia.

We'd been participating in a weekend retreat for the men of our parish, and it had just wrapped up. But on this Sunday afternoon, as the participants left to return to the bustle of the city and their ordinary routines, my friend and I wanted to pause and simply be in God's presence for a little while longer before hitting the road toward home.

So, we walked the easy path to this hidden spot and sat on the sun-warmed stone to gaze at the lush green valley below and around us. It was sunny, though enormous puffy clouds occasionally dimmed the solar blaze. A faint breeze embraced us.

To the right, we could see the large wooden cross bearing witness to the valley from another hilltop within the campgrounds. Ahead of us, we could catch glimpses of the nearby llama farm.

Other than the bleats of the llamas, the soothing swish of tree leaves dancing in the breeze, and the occasional birdsongs, all was quiet.

This is a holy place, I thought, remembering this passage from Exodus. I pulled off my hiking boots. My friend sensed my purpose and did the same. Then we stretched out on the warm rock face and prayed for each other and our loved ones.

Maybe you've experienced a holy place like that. Moses's holy ground probably didn't look all that special—more like a rocky place on a hillside than a spot for sacred encounter. Moses had been minding his own business as a shepherd when God beckoned to him through the astonishing sight of a scrub bush that flamed with fire without being consumed.

And yet there was a limit God gave Moses. To come too close would mean being consumed by the glory of God. For Moses's own protection, God held him back.

On that rocky hillside, God's fiery holiness made the earth and stone pure and holy and glorious. God's perfect presence redeemed the creation.

But Moses had been wandering among the dust and dirt of idolatrous humanity. Those soiled sandals had to be removed so God could deal directly with the tender, obedient heart. Cleansing it. Filling it. Releasing it from pain and fear and uncertainty to find its destiny in the will of God.

Mighty things happen when we acknowledge the holy presence of God. During a personal retreat a few years later, I returned alone to that same rocky outcropping at Camp Mikell. I sat in the same place my friend and I had been so long before, sketched the scene on a pad with a pen, and drank in the view and the presence of God all around me.

And again, I removed my hiking boots.

Once again God had powerfully met me during that personal weekend retreat, the first I had taken by myself. God remained faithful, calling me to take fresh steps of faith, nudging me to trust fully as I took those steps.

During that weekend, God broke through to shatter my complacency, spurring me to think outside the box of my own life plans, softening my heart to allow the Spirit to work. As I never had before, I sensed Jesus's embrace, almost a physical presence, as I surrendered to him. I didn't know what the future held for me, but I did know I was ready for God to lead me into it.

Once again, that mountainside had become holy ground for me.

Where is your holy ground? It's wherever you sense God's presence. It might be a rocky hillside or a peaceful valley. Or perhaps where you are right now is your holy place because you sense God is there with you, as a burning bush or a gentle breeze or a tender touch.

Remove your shoes and worship. Listen to God's Spirit wooing you. Mighty things can happen through you because of this encounter with the holy.

❦

God, I sense you with me now. Your Spirit burns within my heart. You call me into your holy presence. I worship you. I kneel before you. I trust you. Amen.

14. Breaking Out

> Then the LORD said to Moses, "Go down and
> warn the people not to break through to the
> LORD to look; otherwise many of them will
> perish. Even the priests who approach the LORD
> must consecrate themselves or the LORD will
> break out against them." —EXODUS 19:21-22

God beckoned Moses up the holy mountain. In fact, verse 20 explains, God *descended* to the top of the mountain and called Moses *up* to the top of the mountain. They met halfway.

But as soon as Moses reached the peak, God told him to go back down to the plain with a warning, to make sure the people didn't break through attempting to get a look at God.

Face it: if you knew God was coming near, wouldn't you want to do everything you could to try to catch a glimpse? Wouldn't the awesome spectacle intrigue you? Wouldn't the weighty glory attract you?

Of course. But like a moth to a bug zapper, the results would have been devastating. The people weren't ready to behold the sheer holy glory of the God of hosts. Even the priests, those set apart for God's service, had to go through intricate preparations of body, mind, and heart in order to approach God. Otherwise, God's holiness would "break out against them."

The phrase "break out" has the same root as the word used to describe what happened to King David's servant Uzzah. Presuming to steady the holy ark of the covenant to keep it from falling as it was carried by wagon over rough roadways back to Jerusalem, Uzzah reached out and touched it. God's holiness "broke out" and struck poor Uzzah down.

Even though Uzzah meant well, he forgot that approaching God is serious business. Deadly serious. In our casual, easygoing culture, this reality doesn't fit our picture of God. We consider God to be our spiritual friend, heavenly parent, and divine counselor—perhaps even our invisible good buddy we can just hang out with. And in some ways, God is all those things.

But in adopting that easygoing image, we lose sight of the almighty, ineffable holiness of God, a holiness that requires cleansing and preparation before we can even think of entering into God's presence.

God specified to the Israelites the precise ways to prepare for entering this holy presence. And if they didn't get it exactly right...boom! God would "break out."

Let that thought settle in a bit. It's uncomfortable to think about, isn't it? Surprising, even scary. Where is the love? Where is the acceptance? How on earth are we supposed to approach this apparently unapproachable, threatening, all-powerful God without getting zapped into oblivion like a bug on a Southern backyard patio?

Thanks be to God, the way has been provided for us through Christ Jesus. In Christ we are forgiven and cleansed, set free from the bonds that keep us under the threat of holy horror. In Christ we are covered and imbued with righteousness. We become holy, as holy as God is, even to the extent that God's Holy Spirit is comfortable enough to dwell within us.

Still, God can "break out" today. In you. Through you. It's the radical, magnanimous, overpowering outbreak of love—for you and for others around you.

When we are in right relation with this powerfully holy God, we become a channel of that outbreak into a world that so desperately needs God's touch.

Child of God, God's holy presence is within you. Don't keep it bottled up. Let it break out to those around you.

God, I realize that I am in desperate need of your holiness, your very presence. Thank you for cleansing me through Christ— for making me whole and holy. Use me as a channel for your regenerating presence to others today. Amen.

15. A Higher Standard

> You shall not cheat in measuring length,
> weight, or quantity. You shall have honest
> balances, honest weights, an honest ephah,
> and an honest hin: I am the LORD your God,
> who brought you out of the land of Egypt.
> —LEVITICUS 19:35-36

God values justice, honesty, and integrity. For today's
business world—encompassing mega-corporations and
small storefronts—God offers a refreshingly direct and clear
invitation: *Be honest. Do not cheat.*

As Proverbs 11:1 explains, "A false balance is an abomination
to the LORD, but an accurate weight is his delight." God hates
cheating in business dealings, and God loves a transparent,
honest marketplace.

Of course, in the time of Moses there was no official standards
of weights, no Better Business Bureau. It was everyone for
oneself. So cheating was rampant in the marketplace. You just
expected it...and tried your best to cheat back.

It reminds me of a cartoon I once saw taped to the scale in
a supermarket meat department. On the scale lay several

good cuts of meat, along with the butcher's thumb pushing downward, hidden from the customer, while on the other side of the counter the customer's finger pushed upward on the scales, unbeknownst to the butcher. Both their faces appeared angelically innocent.

God sets a higher standard for us—a holy standard. God's people are to use accurate weights and measures, which implies that we are to follow through on our promises, fulfill orders fully, keep our word, live with honesty and authenticity in every area of life. Doing so reflects the character of the God we serve.

What's sad is that this is even an issue. Sure, the business world has always generated scams. A friend of mine once expressed frustration over several years of legal problems resulting from a swimming pool ineptly installed in his back yard. Not only did the pool end up sinking, cracking, and leaking, but it also took months to finish the installation in the first place. Eventually a major collapse sent pool water rushing into a neighbor's yard—and house—resulting in expensive repairs my friend had to cover.

It turned out that the pool installer had created similar havoc all over the region, starting many more pool installations than he could possibly handle in a scheme to "corner the market." Many of the projects never got finished, and those that did resulted in just as many problems as my friend had. Of course, the perpetrator skipped town and was never heard from again.

Local TV news programs frequently air reports of traveling repairmen ripping off elderly homeowners with shoddy or incomplete repairs. One station revealed through hidden cameras that area automobile oil change shops often didn't change the oil at all. Disgruntled customers rant against internet spam that promises improved health with some expensive capsules of worthless ingredients. Dishonest insurance salespersons or bankers or stockbrokers take their clients' money and run. There's no excuse for such larceny.

But what about taking twenty extra minutes on your lunch hour that you don't make up after work? Or "borrowing" office paper, pens, and tape for your kids' homework projects? What about the padded expense report? Or shading the truth regarding your product's capabilities when trying to snare a new account? Or "forgetting" to report some untraceable income on your tax return? What about over-promising and under-delivering?

God delights in fairness and honesty in all our dealings with others.

I learned a lot about integrity in business from a former employer who owned and managed a small advertising agency. In any problem or misunderstanding with clients, Larry always did what was right—and then some.

When a printed brochure had to be trashed because it included a glaring typographical error (which was my department, alas), he ate the cost of reprinting a corrected version—even though the client had reviewed and signed off on the final proofs, error and all. When outside photography costs would come in under what he'd estimated, he would reduce the invoice to reflect the actual expense rather than letting it slide and increasing his profit. Time after time, Larry did what was fair and just, even though it cost him.

Well, it may have cost him dollars, but he experienced God's delight in abundance.

Let's let God's Spirit of holy honesty permeate our life. Then we'll experience God's delight as well.

God, you have beckoned me to a holy standard, a fairer and more just way of living. Equip me to obey, to be honest and evenhanded. I want to enjoy your delight. Amen.

God Beckons You to Obedience

(The Ten Commandments)

16. A Divine Monogamy

> You shall have no other gods before me. You
> shall not make for yourself an idol, whether in
> the form of anything that is in heaven above,
> or that is on the earth beneath, or that is in the
> water under the earth. You shall not bow down
> to them or worship them; for I the LORD your
> God am a jealous God, punishing children
> for the iniquity of parents, to the third and
> the fourth generation of those who reject me,
> but showing steadfast love to the thousandth
> generation of those who love me and keep my
> commandments. —EXODUS 20:3-6

This, obviously, is a command we are to obey. But it is also an invitation. It is God beckoning us into a loving relationship, a divine monogamy.

Yet I wonder why God had to make this the very first of the Ten Commandments. Why did the Israelites keep choosing the wrong path instead of worshiping and serving the One True God?

When Moses proclaimed this command, the Israelites were surrounded by a plethora of gods, usually taking an animal form, typically cruel and bloodthirsty, terrorizing their deluded believers. These gods were made by human hands and therefore utterly powerless. And yet, the Israelites constantly ran after them in a futile attempt to find something better.

Whether the false god they worshiped was a fish or a bull or a bird or even some sort of demon, what could they have gained from it other than some deluded sense of power or self-determination? How would they have benefited? What was their reason for serving a handmade knickknack that held them captive to fear?

Why not instead pursue a relationship with *the* God, the One who rules the universe? The One who expresses unyielding love and limitless care, who is committed to providing for every need, who promises an everlasting kingdom? The One who genuinely communicates with them, beckoning them to a full, meaningful, and—yes—obedient life? The One who would be jealous—unyieldingly loyal—to those who chose to love in return?

Which would you choose? To me the choice is obvious. Simple. Clear.

No other gods for me, only God.

And then, I turn my eyes away from that God I just committed myself to and look at the new job that could bring me more wealth. Or the person who I hope can meet my needs better. Or the financial opportunity that I think can take care of all my wants. The reckless pursuit that promises to ease my pain or the new car that I believe can make me feel more important, more accepted, cooler.

I turn away from God to some other false, handmade, powerless token.

Some other empty promise.

Some other god.

God invites us: *No other gods. Only me.*

❧

God, I hear your invitation to loyal commitment—to a relationship that matters. I want to obey. Make me mindful of the times I choose to worship other things—empty, powerless, useless things—rather than you. Amen.

17. Calling Out to God

You shall not make wrongful use of the name of
the LORD your God, for the LORD will not acquit
anyone who misuses his name. —EXODUS 20:7

❧

Here is another command for us to hear and live into, one that
reveals the degree to which God desires our reverence and our
sober acknowledgment of who God is.

This divine imperative compels us to consider our use of God's
name. Not to take it lightly. Not to consider it useless or
meaningless. Not to toss it off nonchalantly, or worse, in
a curse.

Why? What's the big deal about misusing God's name?

If we use God's name lightly, its connection with the almighty
being we're referring can become weak and shaky. We
disconnect ourselves from the power source, something like a
cell phone moving outside a working cell.

Though cell signals are stronger now, I used to get a slightly
perverse kick watching other passengers riding the MARTA
train from the Atlanta airport to their homes or businesses
after a flight. As people get on the train, many pull out their

cell phones and make a call. The train travels above ground for a few stops and then plunges under downtown Atlanta for several more miles. And with the descent into underground darkness, cell phones would lose their signal, cutting off the conversations. Suddenly I'd hear several people around me muttering, "Hello? Hello?" The spotty service has prompted many a passenger to break this very commandment.

A similar phenomenon occurs when we flippantly use God's name, disconnecting in our own soul the name itself from the One named. Then, when we seriously use the name, when we call out to God, we feel a separation. The line is full of static— or dead. The reality of God's presence is remote because we haven't been taking God seriously.

"God" has become to us just another casual word, and so our relationship *with* God becomes just as casual and unimportant.

No, God says. *Please don't. Instead, revere my name. Take it seriously. Don't cheapen it with casual misuse.*

Make God's name mean something to you. Use it to call out to God, to worship, to adore, to praise, to sing, to pray, to share.

Keep your connection strong and alive.

God, I want to honor you as God—God of the universe, God of my life. Keep me sensitive and reverent. I want to ensure the connection between us is open and strong. I know you'll do your part; help me do mine. Amen.

18. The Wisdom of Rest

Remember the sabbath day, and keep it holy.
For six days you shall labor and do all your
work. But the seventh day is a sabbath to
the LORD your God; you shall not do any
work—you, your son or your daughter, your
male or female slave, your livestock, or the
alien resident in your towns. For in six days
the LORD made heaven and earth, the sea, and
all that is in them, but rested the seventh day;
therefore the LORD blessed the sabbath day and
consecrated it." —EXODUS 20:8-11

❧

I grew up when Blue Laws were common. They required
the closing of virtually all commercial businesses on Sunday.
And my parents, good Methodists that they were, enforced
their own additional Blue Laws. For instance, I knew that if
I managed to avoid cutting the grass on Saturday, I wouldn't
have to mow on Sunday. Smart kid.

On the other hand, one of the most painful experiences of my
youth came out of my folks' desire to observe the sabbath. I
was briefly infatuated with a cute blonde in our church youth
group and one Sunday afternoon was hanging out with her

and a few other friends from church. A spontaneous group decision emerged to go to the downtown theater to catch a movie. I stopped by my home on the way to get some money and permission and was frankly blindsided when my mom informed me that I could not go see a movie on a Sunday.

As my friends drove off without me, I was fuming and embarrassed, my heart crushed by what I considered a ridiculous restriction. Now, of course, I can see the wisdom in the decision—and wish I could exercise it more often with a proper perspective these days.

Over the years, Blue Laws have pretty much disappeared from the books, and Sunday has become just another day in our society. The few hold-out Blue Laws forbidding the purchase of alcohol on Sunday persisted until just recently.

With these restrictions gone, it may be harder than ever to set apart the one day of the week God has called holy—a day to rest in God's presence and focus on our relationships with God and one another.

Now it's up to us to be careful to observe sabbath.

Of course, the original sabbath was Saturday, and Jews still observe that day. But early on, Christians, in recalling the glory of Easter day, transferred the day of rest to Sunday as a way to recall the glory of Easter day week after week.

But the sabbath has become just another weekend day to catch up with all the to-dos. Get some work done around the house. Take the kids to all their sports venues. Run the errands that the busy workweek has prevented from being checked off our list.

And yet without rest, our souls are left exhausted.

God, I now realize, designed the sabbath not as a restriction but as an invitation. The Hebrew word speaks of an intermission from the routine designed for repose.

God beckons us to take time to pray, to meditate, to just *be*. God yearns for us to gather with our siblings in worship and fellowship, in learning and contemplation. God desires that we spend some time with ourselves, with our family, and especially with God.

Jesus made it clear: the sabbath exists not for God's sake but for our own. It is an opportunity for rest and renewal. It is an invitation to communion and contemplation. The sabbath indeed is a way God can heal and strengthen our souls made weary by six days of life in this cold, hard world.

Are you getting the rest and re-creation you need? Take some time today to reflect on how you can set aside a day each week for renewal in the presence of God. Then do it.

God, help me obey your call for a day set aside to focus on you, by myself and with my fellow believers. Give me the wisdom to prioritize and reorganize my activities so I can live in obedience. And thank you for the refreshing renewal you promise as a result. Amen.

19. The Blessing of Giving Honor

Honor your father and your mother, so that
your days may be long in the land that the
LORD your God is giving you. —EXODUS 20:12

A fair number of parents have used this verse to inflict some
loving parental guilt on their children. I will plead the Fifth.

Ironically, the root word behind honor speaks of heaviness,
in both a positive and negative way. It can mean heavy as in
burdensome or dull, but it can also mean heavy as in wealthy,
rich, weighty, important.

I'm sure most of us can identify with both meanings at times.

But this commandment comes with a promise. When we value
our parents, when we consider their love and care for us as
important and meaningful, when we esteem them and revere
them as a God-given source of wisdom and provision, then
our lives will be rich and full.

Of course, not all parents accept God's invitation to raise
their children in life-giving ways. You may have strongly
negative feelings about your parents because they abused you
emotionally or even physically. Even so, your parents gave you

life, so they deserve at least your prayers. And hopefully, some day, your forgiveness, deserved or not.

Regardless of the sort of parents we have, most of us rebelled against them to some degree as a way of separating ourselves and becoming more autonomous. I'm no different, though my rebellion as a youth was relatively tame.

Still, some years ago, I came to appreciate my late parents' values and beliefs once again, thanks in part to the gift of hindsight. As a young adult, I took a self-inflicted journey away from grace, leaving my Methodist upbringing for the dry judgmental desert of conservative evangelical Christianity as a way, I later came to realize, to avoid dealing with my God-given identity as gay. I finally came to understand that my parents' occasional disapproval of my life decisions arose out of their concern that I become my own person, to be sure, but also happy, balanced, fulfilled, and secure.

For the last years of their lives, I sought to honor them by keeping in better touch, listening to them, telling them I love them, and visiting them when I could—particularly during the last year or two they were alive. I never appreciated them more than I did then. I treasure the memory of those precious visits. I miss my folks dearly now.

And now that my own children are adults, I certainly understand that parental concern. It's one thing to be concerned about the safety of young children. But when they are older, the choices potentially have much more serious consequences—even of life and death.

It's not always easy, and I struggle with this continually, but I want to honor my children's freedom and encourage their growth and fulfillment. When I do, they much more readily give me the honor this divine imperative speaks of in return.

And that makes life more worth living for all of us in the land God has given us.

❦

God, give me wisdom and understanding to enable me to honor my parents in positive, appropriate ways. Above all, help me to honor you, the source of all wisdom and goodness and love. Amen.

20. Positive Negatives

You shall not murder. You shall not commit
adultery. You shall not steal. —Exodus 20:13-15

⬥

Simple. Clean. Direct.

Three commandments. Three negative imperatives setting
forth basic rules regarding one's relationships with others.

These rules are captured in just a few words in a few verses,
and yet libraries of books could be written recounting the
painful, devastating human history that has resulted from
willfully breaking them, ignoring them, or casually slipping
away from them.

You may read these words and nod smugly. You've never
killed anybody or broken marriage vows, and maybe the
insignificant theft in your youth can be chalked up to mere
rambunctiousness.

Others have suffered dire consequences of breaking these laws.
They have discovered firsthand that these are important values
upon which civilization rests.

And yet, Jesus says we're all guilty. In the Sermon on the Mount (see Matthew 5), he contends that even thinking about murdering someone, or lusting in your heart over another, or considering what it would be like to have something that's not yours, is just as serious a breach of God's will as the actual act itself.

So, what do we do with this?

God's purpose is not necessarily to make us feel guilty but to give us boundaries that provide safety and security.

They're not restrictions so much as revelations of true freedom.

And Jesus isn't trying to load us up with feelings of powerlessness over our own lusts but to force us to look to him for help, for relief, for true power.

We all miss the mark. We all, whether imprisoned for our errors or not, have broken these commands time and again to one degree or another. While these commandments point to our absolute inability to obey them by ourselves, they also point to the complete provision God has given us through Christ to satisfy them.

They speak an invitation: Come closer.

Know that you are forgiven and cleansed by God.

Receive the power God alone can give to live a healthy, positive life.

Experience within these protective boundaries the true fulfillment and shameless freedom and security that only God can give.

❧

God, help me to hear your "no" in a positive light. Help me to lean on Christ and his righteousness, help me to call on the Spirit's power, and help me to stay safe and secure within the boundaries of your love. Amen.

21. A Neighborly No

> You shall not bear false witness against your
> neighbor. —Exodus 20:16

❧

God offers another negative imperative, another simple
command—at least, on the surface: Don't lie about
your neighbor.

We've all known a neighborhood or workplace gossip. We've
seen—maybe even personally experienced—the shocking hurt
inflicted by a false rumor racing around a community.

I had a close friend I'd often have lunch with. We hadn't seen
each other for a while because he'd been out of town for a
week or so visiting relatives, but we arranged to meet for lunch
at a pizza place not far from where he worked.

My friend had taught me a lot about how spiritual brothers
can hug one another, which was a wonderful revelation for
me. One day early in our friendship, I stuck my hand out for
him to shake after we'd spent some time together—a normal
farewell. He looked at my hand then said with a smile,
"We hug."

So, typically, we hugged whenever we met each other and departed, coming and going. But I suppose understandably, in our quick-to-judge society, he often hesitated hugging me whenever we met in a public place outside of church. Still, on that day we hadn't seen each other in a while, so we did a modified half-hug in the parking lot as we walked toward the restaurant, our arms around each other's shoulders.

We laughed our way into the restaurant and enjoyed our lunch together, catching up on whatever was going on in our lives at the time and afterwards hopped in our cars and headed back to our separate jobs.

The next day in a phone conversation he announced, "No more hugging in public."

"Why?" I asked, more than a bit perplexed.

"Well, there were some people from my work at the pizza place who saw us hugging in the parking lot. We weren't even really hugging, but the word has spread around here like wildfire that I'm gay."

As a single man in his thirties at that time, decades ago, my friend was particularly sensitive to this false assertion. Before I came out some years later, I had never really even considered what people might think of me if they saw me hugging a friend. Still, that unfounded gossip embarrassed and hurt him.

God says don't spread lies or even rumors about your neighbor. Don't start them, don't spread them. Not just about your literal neighbor—that word can refer to any close associate, including a sibling, companion, friend, or spouse.

But there's an underlying truth you'll find when you peel back the surface layer: God invites us to a life of transparency, honesty, and authenticity. Our relationships with all those around us should be built on trust, justice, and charity.

What does that look like?

It means telling the truth even if it hurts. Not avoiding confrontation, not holding back, but telling the truth carefully, honestly, with a view to building up rather than tearing down.

It means not stifling your own difficulties, fears, doubts, or negative feelings but being honest about them and dealing with them positively, on your own or with appropriate help.

It means seeking out others whose words or actions may have hurt you—not to pay them back but to discuss the matter with the goal of reconciliation.

It means living without worrying about posturing, or whether others will accept you, or whether you'll be considered successful or good.

It means just being yourself as God created you.

God calls to you: live the truth. Be the truth.

God, keep me honest. Transparent. Trustworthy. Truthful. In the power of your Spirit. Amen.

22. Heart of the Matter

> You shall not covet your neighbor's house; you
> shall not covet your neighbor's wife, or male or
> female slave, or ox, or donkey, or anything that
> belongs to your neighbor. —Exodus 20:17

I had trouble with this one when I was a kid. But that was really Phil's fault.

Phil lived four houses down from me. All the other homes on our avenue were stately brick, two or three stories with large porches. My house was a Methodist parsonage, but you wouldn't notice much difference between it and all the other homes along the avenue—except for Phil's house. It stuck out like a beautifully manicured thumb: a modern brick ranch with huge windows, a half-moon driveway, and a flawlessly trimmed lawn.

Phil had his own huge bedroom; I had to share mine with one of my brothers. His home had all the most modern amenities—even an automatic dishwasher. He had a color television before just about anyone else did.

But that was nothing. Inside this contemporary home's white-graveled courtyard was a beautiful bronze fountain that shot both water and flame into the air in an amazing elemental dance. You can imagine how impressed my eight-year-old self was at that.

How many games of touch football, baseball, and every form of tag known to humanity did my neighborhood friends and I play in Phil's wide-open yard? How many evenings did we spend chasing lightning bugs in his huge corner lot? How many lazy afternoons did we spend at his house, checking out his latest comic books or playing with his amazing new toys?

Sometimes we'd go camping on wooded property Phil's father owned on the outskirts of town. After an evening of relatively tame and usually harmless adolescent antics, we'd go to sleep around a dying fire in worn-out Boy Scout sleeping bags (except for Phil; his was brand new).

At age 16, when he got his driver's license, Phil's parents gave him a brand-new Jeep. The rest of us had to borrow our parents' definitely uncool old Chryslers and Chevrolets to get around, and even that was a rare privilege.

Oh, how I envied Phil. How I lusted after his possessions. He had everything a boy could ever want or need—and then some. If you had looked in heaven's post office, my mug would have been plastered on the Wanted poster for breaking the Tenth Commandment time and again, because of Phil.

I lost track of Phil in college, but years later I received a letter from my mother. She wrote, "Did I tell you about Phil? His mother would not admit it, but Phil was an alcoholic. Also, he was married to his third wife. His liver shut down, and death followed. It is sad for one so young to die." Phil would have been 43. He was my first childhood friend to die.

This commandment doesn't mean that if you accumulate lots of stuff, God will get you. Rather, God promises that no matter who you are, no matter what you have, God has provided, and will provide, everything you need to be content and fulfilled. You are complete in God. You don't need to envy what someone else has, because if you don't have it, you don't need it.

Can you trust that? Can you believe God?

Phil's tragic life reveals the potential emptiness of all those shiny, nifty things we crave. Sometimes, the things we think will bring us satisfaction are the very things that will keep us from it.

Shift your eyes from your neighbors to your God. And keep them there.

❧

God, my life is complete in you. You are the provider of all that I need. Help me keep my eyes on you, trusting your provision. In this world, that can be a tall order. But you're an all-powerful God. Amen.

God Beckons You
to Intentionality

23. Staying Alert

> Take care and watch yourselves closely, so as
> neither to forget the things that your eyes have
> seen nor to let them slip from your mind all the
> days of your life; make them known to
> your children and your children's children.
> —DEUTERONOMY 4:9

Intentionality.

This is a concept you may hear frequently in the circles of
faith. Being intentional means choosing to do something you
should be doing. Purposefully acting in right ways. Focusing

on what you are called to do at that moment. Being alert and paying close attention to the present moment.

It's a concept I'm always trying to learn myself. I'm often driving in dreadful Atlanta traffic. Many years ago, when I had a commute of 30 miles, it often took well over an hour. Now my commute is a much more manageable four miles, and… it can sometimes take over an hour. It can easily be the most exasperating hour or so of my day. Because when I am going somewhere, I want to be there now.

After driving in Atlanta traffic for some time, I finally realized that I could be more intentional about my commute.

I use the time to pray and talk over things honestly with God—out loud. Sometimes I even cry or yell at God about something. I sing my guts out along with a song I'm streaming. I listen to an audio book I've been meaning to read. I make some phone calls I've been putting off. In recent years I usually listen to the Morning Prayer podcast from Forward Movement.

And sometimes, I simply drive in meditative silence.

It still can be tough to enjoy the commute in a stop-and-go traffic jam, but I am working on intentionally enjoying the journey.

I have even applied the concept of intentionality to such simple tasks as washing dishes. My spouse is a wonderful home chef who loves to entertain friends. I am so blessed to have the best meal in Atlanta on any day of the week right at home. However, he loves to make a mess. "Sorry for the big production," he'll say as I head to the kitchen to do my part, of cleaning up. This is not something I would necessarily choose to do, you understand, particularly cleaning up after a big seven-course dinner with friends.

As I stand at the sink surrounded by food-covered plates, silverware, pots, pans, and serving dishes, I could easily get frustrated and angry and work haphazardly and ineffectively, possibly breaking a few plates and snapping at my spouse in the process.

Or I could choose to be intentional about it.

It's amazing the difference intentionality can make. Feeling the warm water, scrubbing the surfaces, washing away the cleansing soap bubbles, breathing and noticing the breathing.

The Vietnamese Buddhist monk Thich Nhat Hanh was once visited by a friend who was a Catholic priest. The two men shared dinner, then Nhat Hanh said he would wash the dishes before their tea and dessert. The visitor offered to do the dishes while his host made the tea, but the monk said, "Go ahead, but if you wash the dishes, you must know the way to wash them." His friend laughed and assured Nhat Hanh that he did know how. But the monk replied, "There are two ways to wash the dishes. The first is to wash the dishes in order to have clean dishes, and the second is to wash the dishes in order to wash the dishes."[4]

Which way shall we do it? Being intentional about washing the dishes enables me to appreciate the wonderful meal we enjoyed, feel warmed by the love shared around the table, and be thankful for the clean water we have to wash the dishes. It helps me to do a thorough job without rushing through it to get it done. It feels good. It feels right.

Yes, I admit this sounds goofy. But it honestly works. It's something that must be done, so I might as well do it right.

What happens if we apply this concept of intentionality to the larger issues of life? Our relationship with our spouses and children, if we have them. Our friendships. Our colleagues at work. Our church. Even our relationship with God.

Life is rich with responsibilities. We have a calling of God to fulfill. We can choose to approach it around the edges, perfunctorily. We can make a half-hearted effort when we feel like it. Or we can take it head on—attack it directly. We can do our best to keep our hearts from wandering. To stay focused and alert. To keep our calling always at the forefront of our mind.

As I think back about my parenting experience, I sense some chagrin, if not shame. It is so easy to get sidetracked or distracted from the precious time we have with our children by the urgent needs of work or bill-paying or housekeeping or civic responsibilities or friendships or even hobbies. I can feel now how unintentional I was at times with my children.

What if we take this holy invitation to heart? What if we become more alert and vigilant to love and lead and teach our children or other beloved people? What if we purposefully keep fresh in our memory the ways God has worked so faithfully in our lives, meeting our needs, surprising us with unexpected blessings? What if we take care to purposefully seek more ways to be with our family, individually and together, and do some of the things they want to do with us rather than pursuing our own agenda?

Sure, I did the fatherly things. As a good Christian parent, I was careful to check off the major responsibilities with my kids. But looking back, sometimes it feels like that's just about all I did—check them off. I was distracted by so many other things going on in my life; some of them important, but many not so.

Ah, but I still have grandchildren to practice this verse on. And it's amazing how intentional I can be with them if I choose to.

You see, it's all about balance and focus. We will always have a myriad of responsibilities. But we can take them one at a time and focus.

Be alert. Keep close watch. Stay vigilant. God has something for each one of us to do today, right now.

And it will be worth telling our children and grandchildren about.

❦

God, you have called me to fulfill various responsibilities. Help me do so with intentionality, balance, and focus. Help me give every task my utmost. You didn't hold back your love and grace, and I don't want to hold anything back either. Amen.

24. A Word to Remember

Then the LORD said to Moses, "Write this
as a reminder in a book and recite it in the
hearing of Joshua: I will utterly blot out the
remembrance of Amalek from under heaven."
—EXODUS 17:14

I've found that remembering how God has worked in my life requires intentionality. In my utility closet, inside a big plastic bin, I keep several dozen journals of various types and sizes and binding styles. Occasionally I pull one of them out and read a few pages. Memories flood back through my brain as I reread my life notes from a day many years earlier.

This practice started three decades ago when I received a blank book for my thirty-seventh birthday. At the time I was struggling on numerous fronts—including frustrations and burnout in my work and ministry, challenges in my relationships, stagnation in my spiritual life, and an underlying battle over my very identity.

It took me a full week before I finally put pen to the somewhat overwhelmingly blank pages to write the following:

Thursday, 7 a.m.

My new journal beckons, a gift, a symbol of need, an empty, gaping hole waiting to be filled—with words, feelings, prayers, symbolic of the gaping hole in my life also waiting to be filled. A small step, a simple act of applying pen to paper, intended to be a first step in a journey that promises to be difficult yet rewarding, a journey that God only knows where it leads. And though I think I still trust God in that, I think, I still fear it. It is a massive, weighty thing that sits on my chest. I don't want it there, but I don't know how to remove it otherwise.

Small steps: carving out more time in the morning to meditate, write, ponder, pray. I have come to a precipice and stand in confusion and fear. Do I retrace my steps safely backwards? Do I take the rocky path less traveled? Do I jump, not sure whether I have a parachute or not? Or do I just stand there, immobilized, frozen? Today I stand there, but I feel I have turned toward the rocky path. My foot is extended. But I am losing my balance....

God, give me insight. I am so rusty, so crusty, so tired. Freedom beckons. But is it the freedom that is in reality slavery to loneliness, self-imprisonment, and spiritual/emotional death, or is it the freedom of a life lived in the Spirit, in honesty and openness, in truly understanding oneself—the freedom that on its surface seems like captivity to me? I am ready to take a step, I think, but which way?

I read these words today with a sublime detachment. Much has changed in my life since I wrote that. My work is different. I'm an Episcopal priest. Having come out years ago now, I live in a different home with a different spouse. My children are well grown. I seem to have an entirely different set of friends. Even so, some of this still resonates with my much older self.

Yet, I feel more settled in my trust in God. I can see areas where I have grown. I appreciate the difficult, even overwhelming choices I've made—and the sacrificial and often humiliating steps I've been led to take. I am still in desperate need of God's grace and mercy and yet brought so far down the path by God's loving and generous beckoning.

I have my journals to thank for reminding me of the ways I've grown, how God has honed my heart. My journals also force me to face the realization that I am still in process, with a long way to go.

These thoughts about recording the steps of my life come as I read Exodus 17:14. Israel had defeated the Amalekites in the power of God. As long as Moses kept his arms stretched out over the battlefield—assisted by Aaron and Hur who held up his hands—Israel kept winning.

After the battle was won, God directed Moses to write the account of what happened on a scroll, in order for Joshua, and all Israel, to remember it. We can still read the account today in the scriptures. It tells us that God is faithful to provide the strength and wisdom we need to overcome.

Because I've taken the time and made the effort to keep a journal, I find the same lesson between the lines scrawled on those pages. Thank God I have those journals, because it's a lesson I seem to need to be reminded of often.

What can you do to help you remember the things God has done in your life? Today is a good day to begin doing it.

⸿

God, remind me often of the ways you've worked in my life, helping me to grow, coaxing me toward maturity. For any positive step I've taken, I give you the glory, for you are the one who has brought me to this place and will lead me forward. Amen.

25. Immersed in the Word

> This book of the law shall not depart out of
> your mouth; you shall meditate on it day and
> night, so that you may be careful to act in
> accordance with all that is written in it. For
> then you shall make your way prosperous, and
> then you shall be successful. —JOSHUA 1:8

There is no shortage of reading material in my home. In my *sanctum sanctorum*, the small condo in which I live with Dan, next to the living room area is my office—computer, desk, easy chair, and bookcases filled with, well, books. The shelves hold everything from Kierkegaard to Jack Kirby, from devotionals to dime novels.

Surrounding my easy chair are stacks of books, my to-read pile. At the present moment, I'm reading books by Jill Lepore, Jennifer Egan, Walter Brueggemann, Diarmaid McCulloch, and Howard Thurman, among several others. You'll find a Book of Common Prayer and a collection of Flash Gordon Sunday comic strips. And more.

By my bedside now, you'll find the Ken Follett book I'm about to begin and the Van Reid novel I'll read next, plus a reprint collection of all the Batman comic books drawn by Neal Adams. And in my bathroom (yes, I'm a bathroom reader, too) you'll find the latest issues of *Motor Trend, Car and Driver, Vanity Fair, Esquire,* and *AARP Magazine.* And on my Kindle? A whole library of books, classic and modern, mostly yet unread.

Clearly, I am nothing if not wide-ranging in my reading interests. I love books. Books surround me. In addition to the to-read pile beside my chair I have several to-read shelves, which seem to grow exponentially. I can never keep up with my reading. And when I discover a new author whose work resonates with me, as I have lately with John Boyne, I have to get everything they've written. I'll never have time to read all my books, even if I had my Kindle in heaven. Maybe I will, if it's heaven.

One of the most sublime reading experiences I've ever had involved a novel that ultimately became a Pulitzer Prize winner for fiction. Through our mutual interest in the superhero artwork of Jack Kirby, in the 1990s I met the novelist Michael Chabon. He had posted to an email list devoted to Kirby, asking questions about the history of comic books. Having enjoyed his novels, *The Mysteries of Pittsburgh* and *Wonder Boys,* I emailed him to ask if he was the Michael Chabon; indeed, he was. That led to an enjoyable correspondence about writing, faith (Michael and his spouse, the author Ayelet Waldman, are Jewish), and of course comic books.

Michael had joined the Kirby list to do research about the history of comics for his next novel and ultimately asked me (and another fellow on the list who also appreciated Michael's books) to read the manuscript he had just completed, entitled *The Amazing Adventures of Kavalier & Clay*. He wanted feedback, especially on the historical aspects of the story.

Would I!

Before long, an unexpectedly large box containing well over 1,000 typed, double-spaced pages arrived at my doorstep, and I dove in. Oh my, what a rich story full of amazing characters and fascinating history. I don't know if my meager comments helped him in any way to shape the final version as published, but it was an incredible pleasure to read—one of the most enjoyable reading experiences I've known. Plus, my name is right there in the back-of-the-book acknowledgements along with dozens of others far more notable than I am.

Eventually, Michael had to trim more than a fourth of the manuscript, dropping some lovely characters and combining a couple of others into one, to produce a book of a more manageable length. And while the final product is certainly outstanding—well worthy of its Pulitzer Prize—I have to say the earlier manuscript held even more magic for me. I literally could not put the pages down—all 1,000-plus of them.

I think you get the idea that I am a reader. I am always immersed in three to nine or more books at a time.

And, oh yeah, by the way, I read the Bible, too. Somewhere in there.

How about you?

When I read the verse from Joshua, I have to question my reading priorities.

I am immersed in reading, but am I immersed in God's word? Am I intentional about making reading scripture part of my daily routine? Do I think about it, meditate on it, roll it over in my mind and heart and soul? Knock it around, kick its tires, study it in the light of the sun, throw it against the wall and see if it sticks?

God tells Joshua that if he's going to succeed in his efforts for Israel to dwell successfully in the Promised Land, he must meditate on God's word. He couldn't let it out of his mind for a moment.

God invites us to consider the scriptures. Meditate on them. Ponder the words. Be intentional about the practice. Keep them front and center in our conscious thinking.

But let's not stop there. The purpose of meditating on God's word is for us to *do* God's word. To live it out, follow it, make it part of our being. For this to happen requires that we be immersed in it. Saturated by it. Soaking it in.

And this requires time and effort. But God promises a wonderful pay-off for that investment: "Then you shall make your way prosperous, and then you shall be successful."

Are my reading priorities in good order? Have I put first things first? Do I allow myself sufficient time in my waking hours to think about what God is calling me to do, what God is challenging me to be about?

God beckons you and me to be intentional about spending time meditating on the scriptures, to wrestle with what we hear, to question and probe and consider and think through God's word in the indwelling presence of the Spirit.

That's how to "make your way prosperous" today.

❧

God, impress upon me the need to be intentional about reading, knowing, and doing your Word. Guide me through my study; make it real, alive, engaging, effective. Amen.

26. Look Up

> Lift up your eyes and look around; they all
> gather together, they come to you; your sons
> shall come from far away, and your daughters
> shall be carried on their nurses' arms. Then
> you shall see and be radiant; your heart shall
> thrill and rejoice, because the abundance of the
> sea shall be brought to you, the wealth of the
> nations shall come to you. —Isaiah 60:4-5

Have you ever found yourself so intently focused on your internal turmoil, so blinded by suffocating circumstances, that you fail to realize where you are?

I must admit that on more than one occasion while driving on an interstate highway, lost in thought, I have shaken myself out of a reverie to realize I had no idea where I was—or whether I'd missed my exit ramp. Even on my commute to work or back home, sometimes I have to stop and think for a few seconds about which street I am traveling. So far, at least, I haven't forgotten whether I'm coming or going—so perhaps there's hope.

Israel as a nation was in something of the same situation. They had become so inwardly focused, so consumed by their idolatry, so paralyzed by their self-absorbed ignorance of the true way, that they couldn't see beyond their own faces.

God calls to them: lift up your eyes and look around. See what God is doing.

Their sons and daughters are returning to their homeland, pouring back into the land God had given them from every corner of the world, "The wealth of the nations shall come to you." This is God's promise to them, the hope that could quicken their spirits.

Watch and see what God will do. This requires being aware, making the effort, keeping our focus on what's real. It requires looking beyond oneself to the holy horizon.

What we see there will thrill our heart to bursting—because what we'll see is God at work all around us.

❧

God, help me lift my eyes to the horizon, to see you at work, to see your wonderful will unfolding ahead of me. Thank you for the encouragement. Amen.

God Beckons You to Renewal

27. Come to the Waters

> Ho, everyone who thirsts, come to the waters;
> and you that have no money, come, buy and
> eat! Come, buy wine and milk without money
> and without price. —ISAIAH 55:1

Do you take water for granted?

You have easy access to bottled water in your refrigerator, a water fountain or watercooler at work, even kitchen tap water. At the slightest twinge of thirst, it's not difficult to satisfy the craving.

When was the last time you were really thirsty? Maybe it was a hot summer day hiking in the woods with a canteen near empty or on a beach sizzling under the sun, too relaxed to be bothered to grab a chilly, sweaty can of soda. Perhaps you were working outside in biting, dry air, shoveling a thick blanket of snow or finishing a big Easter ham dinner, parched by the salty meat.

Even in those times it didn't require much effort to slake your thirst.

When the Caribbean islands were rocked by hurricanes, one after another, a few years ago, news reports for weeks declared that drinkable water was not available to the folks in the storms' wake. Distributing water was haphazard and difficult. If people did have access to water, they were told to boil it—but most of the citizens had no power to fire up a stove. It was horrifying to contemplate.

Can you remember a time you were dying for a sip of water? Has it been a while since you really yearned for cool liquid to put out the fire in your throat? Do you know what it means to thirst? Really?

While you ponder that question, ask yourself another. What about your spiritual thirst? Are you thirsty for God? Does your dry, dusty spirit yearn for refreshment from God's hand—a fountain of living water bubbling within your soul?

Sometimes we get so involved in our activities that we don't even realize how thirsty we are. So, when we grab that cold water bottle, we're surprised at how good it feels going down.

Many years ago when my grandson was a toddler, he spent a summer Saturday with me. We had gone for a walk and then he played outside in a park. He kept me entertained with his nonstop, inquisitive, full-force investigations of every plant, leaf, and twig he could find. After a while, I offered him a juice bottle. He grabbed it and drank heartily for several minutes, hardly catching a breath.

If he had been aware of his mighty thirst, he was still unable to ask for what he needed, but he gladly took it when offered.

I can certainly identify with that situation. I become so involved in the minutia of daily living that I don't realize how parched my soul really is—until the Spirit grabs hold of me in some surprising way and offers the cleansing, cooling, renewing draft of the holy water of God's presence.

There is nothing more refreshing.

Hear God's clear, cool invitation to you: *Come. Come to the waters. Come, if you are thirsty, to the flowing, bubbling, effervescent fountain of eternal life.*

Renewal flows from God alone. If you are thirsty, even the least bit, for spiritual authenticity, God invites you, welcomes you, yearns for you to come to the waters.

And that's just the start. When we come, wine and milk will flow freely: the wine of the Spirit, the milk of God's mothering love.

Best of all, God's spiritual refreshment costs nothing; it is free. And nothing hinders our way except our stubborn self-will. It is up to each of us to come, receive, and be filled to overflowing with the spiritual refreshment only God can give us.

Ho! All who are thirsty are welcome. Drink deep.

⌘

God, I yearn for your renewing draughts of the water of life. Thank you for the invitation to come to you for your free gift of eternal life. Let me drink deeply. Amen.

28. God's Love Song

Incline your ear, and come to me; listen, so
that you may live. I will make with you an
everlasting covenant, my steadfast, sure love for
David. —Isaiah 55:3

⌘

One of the most beautiful sights is when a mother rocks a
child to sleep, softly singing love songs. The child relaxes
blissfully in the mother's arms, totally satisfied, surrendering to
the needed rest after an eventful day of play.

I think of that warm and wondrous image when I read this
verse about God singing a song of covenant love over us.
In this music of the heavens, God pledges to love us with a
faithful, committed, unyielding, everlasting love—a love far
deeper even than a parent's for a child.

Do you hear God's love song? God desires that you do. This
love, Isaiah tells us, is a "steadfast, sure love." What God said
to Isaiah and David, God says to us. "Incline your ear, and
come to me; listen, so that you may live." In other words, pay
attention to the Spirit's whisper. Come closer to God. Rest in
God's arms. And experience genuine renewal.

I witnessed the power of God's love song one Sunday morning in the first Episcopal church I was involved in. They had a powerful prayer ministry. During the prayers of the people, the leader offered an opportunity for people in the congregation to speak out a word, phrase, sense, or image that God's Spirit brought to mind. These images ranged from "I see an image of a flowering tree" to "pain in the shoulder" to "a burning stick" or "a wheat field."

If someone sensed that one of those words or images had meaning to them, they could consider it as an invitation from God to come for prayer after taking communion. For instance, one morning, a member in the choir said, "A slice of Swiss cheese." There were some chuckles at that one, but since I had actually had a slice of Swiss cheese for breakfast that morning—the first and only time in my life I think I had ever eaten such for breakfast—I took that as a sign that God was inviting me to come for prayer.

After receiving the bread and the wine, you could walk to the baptistry area along the side of the nave and join a prayer team of two or three folks. They would simply invite you to focus on God, open your hands and heart to receive whatever God might have for you. The prayer team would stand with you, praying for you silently and watching as God went to work.

One Sunday morning when I was serving on the prayer team, a woman who was clearly in emotional despair approached.

I wondered if she could even focus her mind in prayer, she seemed so disturbed and tense. She explained that one of the words someone had spoken out—something that probably meant nothing to the person who said it—had resonated.

While we prayed silently for her, she stood there, a seeming wad of pain and fear. While the rest of the congregation continued to receive communion, the choir began to sing the hauntingly beautiful old hymn, "There is a balm in Gilead…to soothe the sin-sick soul." Immediately my prayer partner and I could sense the peace and presence of God infusing the woman, her muscles relaxing, her nerves untangling. Tears came to her eyes, a smile to her face, a glow to her countenance.

After a few moments of experiencing the loving, healing, reassuring presence of God, she blinked a few times, her face beaming, and said, "I am loved after all. I didn't even realize I needed that reassurance until God invited me to receive it." She hugged us and added, "That hymn they sang was my mother's favorite—she used to sing it to me all the time when I was a child." Smiling, she returned to her seat.

On that morning years ago, that woman paid attention to God's wooing to her. And because she did, she heard the heavenly love song of grace and forgiveness.

When we hear this love song, God lights a fire of renewal in our soul that cannot be extinguished by the wind, but only roars hotter, purer, with life and light and energy in that wind of the Spirit.

Its warmth spreads to everyone around you.

God's love gives life and nourishes the soul. Forever.

Can you hear it? God beckons you to come closer. And listen carefully.

❧

God, I am heeding your invitation to come close, to listen carefully, to hear your loving, life-giving, spirit-renewing words. Thank you for your sure, solid, everlasting love. Amen.

29. Arise and Shine

Arise, shine; for your light has come, and the
glory of the LORD has risen upon you.
—ISAIAH 60:1

⟨∞⟩

When you are weighed down by guilt or shame...

When you are overwhelmed by the increasingly difficult
burdens of living...

When you are utterly absorbed in worry and fear and
uncertainty...

When you are reeling in the pain of rejection or abuse...

When you find yourself in those places, it feels almost
impossible to wake up. To get out of bed. To look up. To
experience life at its fullest. To shine.

Yet this was God's invitation to Israel. They had been rejecting
God's generous beckoning for generations and had suffered
significantly for their selfish shortsightedness.

God, through the prophet Isaiah, called them to shake off that
ingrained despondency.

Wake up. Get out of bed. Shake the sleep out of your head, the pain off your aching limbs. Breathe in the new day to the depths of your being. Face the bright morning, God pleads to Jerusalem—and to you.

Receive God's renewing light. Feel its warmth, experience the healing it brings. And shine.

What is light? It is God's blessing. Joy. Wisdom. Salvation. Restoration. Feel its warmth, experience the healing it brings. This light is the reality of God's perfect, all-encompassing presence in your soul. It is always there, shining. But you must be awake to sense it.

Just as God did through Israel, God shines the light on us so we can in turn shine God's light on the world. When that channel is open, the world turns to God.

Hear God's invitation. Sense the Spirit's stirring within you. Receive God's luminous blessing on your life, so you can in turn bless the world around you.

It is a decision of your will, a turning of your face toward the Son, purposefully sensing and receiving the warmth and light. And then reflecting that light to others.

When we open our hearts to the love of God, it softens our hardened hearts and banishes our burdens, pains, and fears.

God's bright glory has risen. For you.

Arise. Shine!

⤖

God, you beckon me to rise, get out of bed, feel the warmth of your light on my face, and be renewed. Give me the strength to heed your welcome—to receive your blessing so I can in turn reach out and be a blessing to someone else. Amen.

God Beckons You
to Fulfillment

30. Walking Forward

> You must follow exactly the path that the LORD
> your God has commanded you, so that you
> may live, and that it may go well with you, and
> that you may live long in the land that you are
> to possess. —DEUTERONOMY 5:33

Doesn't everybody want a good life? Doesn't everyone want
to live long in a good place? Certainly. And this verse makes
it sound as though all you have to do is to obey God's
commands— "follow exactly the path that the LORD your God
has commanded"—and you will be blessed and fulfilled.

I think you and I are experienced enough in this thing called life to know it doesn't always work that way. We can obey every single command of God we can think of, and then some, and still suffer loss, want, tragedy, emptiness, sorrow, and pain.

So why does Moses taunt us this way? Why does he make it sound so easy? Why does God set us up for disappointment like this?

Or...do you feel guilty asking? A little ashamed that you are not as blindly thankful as you should be, even though you're not being blessed as lavishly as God seems to promise here?

This is where a little maturity, some hard-won experience, can come in handy.

Our responsibility is to walk the path God has put before us. This road may have some occasional hills to climb or potholes to avoid, some confusing intersections to negotiate. But walk it. Walk straight ahead on it. And then trust God for whatever happens. Because God is walking along with you.

Following the path toward uncertainty brings to mind an experience I had in my youthful career as a journalist, working for Jim Comstock at *The West Virginia Hillbilly* weekly newspaper. One Thursday morning in August 1977, I reported to work at 7:30 a.m. to find Comstock already banging away at his manual typewriter, the *Today* show blaring away in the background.

"Pete," Jim barked in that urgent, high-pitched voice of his, "some coal miners are marching on Washington tomorrow. I want you to cover it."

I had my orders, so I was off in my '72 Ford bound for Washington, D.C., 300 or so miles away, a city I had visited twice in my life—once as a youngster on a family vacation and again for two weeks during high school with a half dozen pals in a pilot program sponsored by my congressman (a program we must have ruined because he never did it again).

I had no idea where or when the miners' march was supposed to be. I didn't even have a map of Washington. I had no place to stay once I got there. I did figure out which highway to drive on to get there, though.

The morning paper reported that about a thousand miners—who were on a wildcat strike at the time, mad at both the owners and their own union—were heading to Washington in 20 Greyhound buses to try to draw attention to their plight and push for a congressional investigation.

As I drove toward the nation's capital, my apprehension rose. How in the world would I know what to do or where to go? I was still a very green journalist, and, having worked on the *Hillbilly*—not exactly a real newspaper—for only a year or so, I hadn't had many dealings with actual news stories.

About an hour or so outside of Washington, in Northeastern Virginia, I was trying to figure out my game plan. Actually, I started praying in earnest. It was getting to be early evening by now. I figured I could sleep in my car in downtown Washington (though I could see the headlines screaming about what might happen if I did) and pick up a D.C. newspaper to find out about the march. I didn't have much money, but I could get by. I had my trusty black-and-white Polaroid camera to snap some photos, along with a legal pad. That's all I needed. Right?

As the highway stretched on, it suddenly occurred to me that my oldest brother Greg lived at that time in Annapolis, Maryland, and wasn't that near Washington? Maybe I could stop somewhere and give him a call, at least say, "Hey."

I was ruminating on that when out of the corner of my eye I spotted a purple Triumph TR-7 speeding by me in the left lane. Funny, I thought, Greg has a car just like that. I wonder…? Nah. I'm an hour west of Washington. He lives in Annapolis. Couldn't be him.

But it wouldn't hurt to check. So, I pulled my trusty Ford into the passing lane and accelerated to try to catch up with that sports car again. Within seconds I was running parallel to the Triumph.

My jaw dropped in exuberant shock: there in the sports car next to me were my brother and his wife.

I honked and waved and carried on, nearly losing control of my car with the shock of the discovery. I can still remember the look on my brother's face—as if to say, what is this idiot driver next to me doing? He's going to get us both killed carrying on like that!

Then recognition hit his face. We pulled over and hugged each other, asking each other what the heck each of us was doing there of all places.

It turned out Greg and Dora were heading home from her family reunion in Kentucky. When I told them what I was doing, they insisted I follow them home. And it turned out Annapolis is right close to Washington. So, I had a nice spare bed to sleep on, a good breakfast, and great company. And their morning paper spelled out everything I needed to know about the miners' march. Greg even gave me a map of Washington, D.C., so I could find McPherson Park, where the miners would rendezvous before their march.

I've always enjoyed looking back on that experience and telling others about it. After all, the odds of our meeting along the interstate highway must be astronomical. And when I think of how it could have turned out, I remind myself that there is a God: a God who cares, who blesses in unusual ways, who fulfills our needs, who satisfies our longings, and who promises to be with us on the straight journey of obedience.

God, help me to walk straight on the road you set before me. Help me to keep walking, even in uncertain times, knowing that you're walking with me, and that you promise to bless me. Amen.

31. Turning Toward Life

> Turn to me and be saved, all the ends of the
> earth! For I am God, and there is no other.
> —ISAIAH 45:22

❧

It doesn't matter who we are, or where we are, or what our circumstances may be: God invites us, yearns for us, to turn and face God. For there is no other.

Experiencing true fulfillment in the life God beckons us to live requires coming closer, surrendering, giving up our own direction, our own solutions. Coming closer means taking our eyes off our own resources, our pet possessions, our well-constructed self-protective devices, and turning, facing—looking right at—God.

It's an imperative. A command. An invitation.

The imperative "turn to me" is so simple, so pure. And yet it's so astonishingly difficult. We resist it. Our stubbornness keeps our neck aimed in the wrong direction, away from this God who yearns for us.

But what would happen if we did turn and look to God?

We will be helped. We will be saved.

Isn't that what we yearn for? Isn't that what we desperately chase around for? Aren't we driving ourselves to exhaustion with our cravings for it? And yet the invitation stands.

The word saved has, unfortunately, become a bit of a misunderstood cliché in the Christian faith. The Hebrew root, *yasha*, has some refreshing nuances. The wise and hoary *Strong's Concordance* defines this word: "to be open, wide or free, that is, (by implication) to be safe; causatively to free or succor… defend, deliver…help, preserve, rescue, be safe, bring salvation…get victory."

Read each of those words slowly and carefully and let the realization of what God is offering us—yes, even you and me—sink in.

Turn to me, God says, *and be open, wide, free, safe, triumphant.*

Only in God—and "there is no other"—can we experience this liberating salvation. Only in God can we find fulfillment for all time and beyond.

What is keeping you from turning, or turning again?

God, I turn to you. I run to you. I lean on you. I trust you and you alone for all the help and salvation I need. Amen.

32. A Bountiful Banquet

> Why do you spend your money for that which
> is not bread, and your labor for that which does
> not satisfy? Listen carefully to me, and eat what
> is good, and delight yourselves in rich food.
> —ISAIAH 55:2

❧

Have you ever attended a really fancy banquet? I don't mean
the rubber-chicken-serving community or church functions.
I mean a banquet with tables groaning under the weight of
rich and mouth-watering delicacies. Fine crystal and expensive
china and exquisite silverware. Crisply attired servers attending
to your every need as though they could read your mind.
Beautiful music performed by a skilled chamber orchestra
providing the perfect ambience for stimulating conversation.

Frankly, such experiences have been rare in my life. But I
did get an opportunity to attend a fancy banquet early in my
journalism career. It was held at The Greenbrier, the world-
famous West Virginia resort. During my newspapering days
with *The West Virginia Hillbilly*, I was invited to a banquet
my boss Jim Comstock was throwing for that year's graduates
of The University of Hard Knocks, attracting a wide range of
business and political luminaries from across the state.

The University of Hard Knocks was a mythical school of higher education that Jim had created to honor men and women who had succeeded in life without the benefit of a college diploma, doing it the hard way, overcoming all obstacles. The school's colors? Black and blue, of course. And every diploma included the school's official seal: a band-aid.

The main event was held in one of The Greenbrier's sumptuous gold-and-marble swathed dining halls. This renowned hotel, tucked among the state's lush green hills, where presidents and other national legends often worked and played and golfed, apparently had more silverware than they knew what to do with, or they were expecting a second shift of diners after us and figured they wouldn't have time to reset the table. There were knives and forks and spoons displayed at all angles around each plate.

It was all quite confusing to me, a green youth not long out of college (as if I would comprehend it much better now).

But I managed to keep my eye on my fellow diners around the circular banquet table with seating for ten, taking cues from them as to which piece of silver to use with which food. What was disconcerting was that I noticed a lot of other people glancing around surreptitiously, so I suppose I wasn't the only one lost in that forest of silver utensils.

In this classically elegant, exquisite, and very proper setting, I sat to the right of a noted company founder and chief executive named Joe, who was also the husband of the founder of the National Grandparents' Day holiday.

The salad, I recall, was wonderfully fresh and tasty. As I chomped on it, I noticed that Joe just sat there while everyone else devoured their salads. Well, I figured, he must not care for salad.

Then I noticed Joe's wife—sitting to his left—was eating his salad. Obviously, she must have loved the salad and, since he wasn't eating his, she would just help herself. But then it dawned on me that the person sitting next to Marian was eating what I assumed was Marian's salad—and such was the case all the way around the table.

Until you came back around the circular table to me. And sitting untouched on the other side of my plate was another salad.

The force of what I had done hit my twenty-one-year-old head like a sledgehammer. *I was eating the salad of one of West Virginia's most prominent business leaders.* I was mortified. What a *faux pas*. Miss Manners would have simply died.

I was so embarrassed I couldn't even offer my own untouched salad to Joe. In fact, I couldn't say another word to him all evening. I was slightly relieved, though no doubt blushing, when the servers whisked away the salad plates.

A week or so later, I wrote Joe a letter about an ad he'd placed in our newspaper and, in a postscript, apologized for eating his salad at The Greenbrier. He graciously wrote back, telling me not to worry—he didn't like salads anyway. Whether or not that was true, it made me feel better.

But if I thought the banquet at The Greenbrier was fancy and sumptuous, I haven't seen anything yet.

Such earthly banquets—extravagant though they may be— fade into insignificance when we consider what God has prepared for you and me. God sets before us every good thing we could possibly imagine, and far more, and patiently waits to serve us. If only we would come.

But we may not even be aware of the feast prepared in our honor, awaiting our enjoyment. We're busy working, doing, moving about, laboring for a crust of hard bread or airy cotton candy.

We pass up even the most basic spiritual nourishment for junk food, and instead fill our cravings with something false and empty and futile, something that looks like it should taste good and fill our bellies with satisfaction, but never can.

Maybe we're full on success in the business world, with money to buy all sorts of expensive toys and "valuable" stuff and status in a world of people always trying to outdo each other. Maybe we sate ourselves with relationships that should soothe old pain and make hearts beat full forever, but oddly never quite do.

There is a lot of junk food around us that we pretend makes for nourishing, filling, satisfying meals. And if one bit of fluff doesn't fill us, we try another.

"Listen carefully to me," God cries to us, holding out an alternative. It is wholesome. Delightful. Rich. Fulfilling. It is the finest. The spiritual feast you and I are invited to in Jesus Christ is an endless and powerful and filling and pure and utterly satisfying banquet. We need only accept the invitation and come to the table.

Your seat is waiting.

God, in my relentless search for fulfillment, help me to reassess in the light of your word the nourishment I spend my time and money on. Help me to come to you instead of to the things that never satisfy. Help me to realize that the banquet you've invited me to holds all the contentment, all the fulfillment, that I could ever hope to receive. Amen.

33. Living as a God-Seeker

> For thus says the LORD to the house of Israel:
> Seek me and live; but do not seek Bethel, and
> do not enter into Gilgal or cross over to Beer-
> sheba; for Gilgal shall surely go into exile, and
> Bethel shall come to nothing. Seek the LORD
> and live, or he will break out against the house
> of Joseph like fire, and it will devour Bethel,
> with no one to quench it. —AMOS 5:4-6

Time after time God graciously, inexhaustibly, extended to
Israel an invitation of mercy. This time it came through the
prophet Amos: "Seek me and live." Come home. Return to
me and be welcomed. Forsake the false and find the true. Turn
from death and experience true, fulfilling, everlasting life.

Yet, time after time, Israel spurned God's gracious wooing.
The people felt they knew how to live more fulfilling and
successful lives than the Creator of that very life did. So, they
wasted their time fooling around with the false, meaningless,
powerless idols of Bethel, Gilgal, or Beer-sheba, with ideas and
approaches to life that were all show and no substance, idols
that were empty and ultimately fruitless.

All God wanted for them, and all God wants from us, is to respond to the merciful invitation before us: "Seek me and live."

What does seeking God look like?

The Hebrew root behind the word seek has the sense of diligence, of habit. It means to frequent a place. To walk around in it. Search carefully in it. *Be* in it.

Seeking God means dwelling in God's presence, making yourself at home in God's way.

Seeking God means keeping God foremost in your thoughts, in your decision-making process, in your relationships with others, in your walk in the world as you fulfill your calling.

Seeking God means searching for ways to serve as a channel of God's love and care to those in need around you, whoever they might be.

Living as a God-seeker is truly living. It takes courage. It requires taking responsibility. It means being deliberate about seeking God and about following God's ways.

But it's worth it, because being a God-seeker is the only way to experience a life of true meaning, fulfillment, purpose, and joy.

⸎

God, give me the courage and intentionality I need to truly seek you, to keep seeking you, to stop looking for fulfillment in empty places. Thank you for continually wooing me into your presence. Here I come. Amen.

II

THE
LOVING SAVIOR
AND YOU

*Jesus's Invitations to You
from the Gospels*

Jesus Beckons You to Follow

1. Taking the First Step

> As Jesus passed along the Sea of Galilee, he saw Simon and his brother Andrew casting a net into the sea—for they were fishermen. And Jesus said to them, "Follow me and I will make you fish for people." And immediately they left their nets and followed him. —MARK 1:16-18

Jesus may have looked like an ordinary beachcomber, walking leisurely along the shoreline. But he had important matters on his mind. He faced choices that would shape the fruitfulness of his work on earth.

Who would join him? Who should walk with him, learn from him, risk with him? Who would be willing to sacrifice their comfortable everyday existence in order to enter a world that required absolute trust in God?

Whom should Jesus choose? And who would choose to follow him?

He was walking, praying, and pondering when he saw two men fishing. They were hard, leathery men, beefy and salty. Their eyes squinted tight into spiderwebs of wrinkles to keep the sunlight that danced off the Sea of Galilee out of their eyes. Their hands were worn, calloused, cracked, and thick from their work—tough, smelly work that paid just enough to keep their livelihood stable.

Jesus approached these two men and gave them a challenge, an invitation to more: "Follow me." He promised to change the way they worked—reaching out to people in Jesus's name rather than casting nets for mere sardines or carp.

Mark reports that they dropped their nets right then. They didn't even think it over. They just followed Jesus.

Did they know what they were doing? Where they might be going?

Were they so burned out by their everyday lives that they jumped at the first invitation to something new and different?

Were they so dissatisfied with the way things were going, with their small life's frustrations and fears, that they leapt at the chance to stretch their boundaries?

Were they so hungry to experience real meaning and purpose in life, to forge real relationships with others, that they couldn't throw their fishing nets away fast enough?

Were they so weary of the same old routines and responsibilities that they were willing to step out into the unknown, guided only by Jesus?

Were they so thirsty for God that they would unhesitatingly leave their safe and stable life and put themselves into God's hands in order to seek others to join them in God's family?

Were they so different from you and me?

No. They were just people. Simple, hardworking, ordinary people. With the same responsibilities and joys and hardships and fears you and I have, just set in a different context of place and time.

Jesus cut a compelling figure. His teachings were bold and gripping, and perhaps they'd been listening to him teach at the edge of the growing crowd. Peter and Andrew had apparently encountered Jesus once already (see John 1:35-42).

Even so, they had to listen to his invitation. And they had to accept it. They had to put aside the nets that tangled their lives, take that first step, and follow.

They were no different from us.

Are you any different from them?

⟨৪৹⟩

Jesus, the people you called were just ordinary people. Like me. But you gave them an extraordinary challenge to follow you. It's the same challenge you give me today. How will I respond to your invitation? Amen.

2. How to Follow Jesus

> He called the crowd with his disciples, and said
> to them, "If any want to become my followers,
> let them deny themselves and take up their
> cross and follow me." —MARK 8:34

Jesus's words fly in the face of everything our culture tells us.

We are supposed to be leaders, taking destiny in our hands and charge forward.

We're supposed to take control of our lives, live it as we think best, and look out for Number One.

We're supposed to do whatever we need to soothe our hurts and deal with our wounds so as to get rid of them.

We should try anything to avoid suffering and pain and conflict and difficulties.

We've earned success and wealth and position and power. We have the right to claim whatever we feel we need from God.

We deserve the best!

We live in a culture that provides endless models for successful living that reflect these crass assumptions—and that seem totally upside down from what Jesus invites us into.

In short, if you intend to be with Jesus, you must let him lead. Let him be in control. Let him run things his way.

And this word is for all his followers—not just his disciples, not just his closest friends, not just the religious leaders, clergy, professionals. It's for everybody. This means not running from difficulties or suffering, not shying away from opposition or persecution. But embracing it.

When you stand up for God's ways, for justice, for righteousness, you will likely raise a ruckus. The complacent people and the controlling people will rebel against such a message. Those who are stuck in their rigid understanding of God's truth will strike back at a message that seeks to overthrow such judgmentalism.

Let Jesus lead, and he might just lead you to the cross.

But, he says, don't hesitate. Don't avoid it. Embrace it. Watch what he does. And follow.

So, what does this mean in the life of a garden-variety follower like you and me? Are we really going to get killed because of our faith?

Not likely. But, when you seek to bring Jesus's loving justice into this world, you might run into all sorts of opposition. You might be shunned. You might even lose a few "friends."

In early 2003, just before the war in Iraq began, the *Day 1* radio program featured beloved Lutheran minister Barbara Lundblad, one of our listeners' favorites, who encouraged each of us, and our nation, to take a hard look at our self-assumed right to be in charge.[5]

Drawing a parallel between Naaman, the mighty warrior who sought to be healed of his leprosy by the prophet Elisha, and the United States, she urged us to assume an attitude of humility, to listen to our neighbors around the world, to seek to obey God's commands even when they made little sense.

We had an unusually high number of requests for sermon transcripts that week—her message struck a deep chord in most listeners. On the other hand, we also received a couple of strident phone calls from good Christians excoriating us for our anti-Americanism, threatening to spread the word about our apparent communism, and telling their friends to withhold any financial gifts to our ministry until we mended our ways. One man called a half dozen times to curse at us for daring to question America's status as the leader of the world in a time of war.

The caller may have missed the point of the sermon, which could have been replayed countless times in the years since it was first broadcast with relevant effect. But his reaction demonstrates how much most of us—on both a personal and a national level—prefer to be in charge, on top and in control. We don't naturally embrace the path Jesus took, the path of humility, justice, and suffering.

Humility is not something we naturally want to do. It's not necessarily "The American Way." But it is Jesus's way. It's the way of life Jesus beckons us to embrace, even if the results may be painful.

By the way—the man who called half a dozen times to curse us out? His final call was one of humble apology. His pastor had encouraged him to settle down and realize that our intentions were honorable, and that while we might disagree on some major issues, we are still brothers in the faith.

That was a beautiful example of letting Jesus lead and of humbly following.

❦

Jesus, sometimes I think I try too hard to understand what it means to follow you. I spend so much time trying to make sense of it that I never get around to doing it. You carried a cross for a purpose. You call me to put my own needs and desires and interests behind your own and follow your example into the unknown. It feels very big. Yet it also feels very simple. It's what I want to do. Help me do it. Amen.

3. One Thing Left

> As [Jesus] was setting out on a journey, a man
> ran up and knelt before him, and asked him,
> "Good Teacher, what must I do to inherit
> eternal life?"… Jesus, looking at him, loved him
> and said, "You lack one thing; go, sell what you
> own, and give the money to the poor, and you
> will have treasure in heaven; then come, follow
> me." —MARK 10:17,21

He seems a well-meaning guy.

He approaches Jesus enthusiastically. He treats Jesus reverently, acknowledging him as a respected teacher. It's clear he seeks to know how to enter into an eternal relationship with God.

What's more, he knows his scriptures. And he tells Jesus he has followed the basic requirements of the faith—the Ten Commandments—since he was a boy (Mark 10:19-20). He hasn't killed anyone, committed adultery, stolen, lied, or cheated, and he honors his father and mother.

Check, check, check, check, check, and check.

Any of us would have taken a good look at this earnest young man and seen a success in the making. He had it all together. He lived the righteous life. He sought the truth.

But Jesus looks right through him, down into his very soul. What he sees causes a mixture of compassionate love and sorrow within the Lord. He must have seen that this young man—at least a significant part of him—wants to be a sincere, dedicated follower of Christ. He might have been one of the most effective disciples ever. His winsomeness, his eager desire to learn, his willingness to follow—Jesus sees it and loves the man. His heart is good.

But it is not a fully open heart, ready to be willingly and fully given over to Jesus. Something is holding this man back, and Jesus sees it in his eyes, deep within his soul. Something that would continually trip the man up from following Christ fully and without hesitation.

Yes, he is doing most everything right. But Jesus says, "You lack one thing; go, sell what you own, and give the money to the poor, and you will have treasure in heaven; then come, follow me."

It is a gentle command, perhaps a test of the man's will. A coaxing of his soul. Clearly, Jesus wants this man's companionship. He wants him to follow. But he also knows this one thing will be an insurmountable obstacle for him, for the young man is apparently too dependent upon his wealth and his possessions to be dependent upon Jesus.

"When [the man] heard this, he was shocked and went away grieving, for he had many possessions" (Mark 10:22). Or perhaps, many possessions had him.

Jesus sees right through us. Jesus drives a hard bargain. Jesus expects a fully devoted heart. His love is a demanding love. A jealous love. But when his love is accepted, it can bring freedom and heavenly wealth. It can lead us on a journey of immeasurable joy and fulfillment.

Jesus looks into your eyes, deep into your heart, and loves you. What's holding you back? Fear, uncertainty, selfishness? Some unhealthy relationships? The allure of pleasure, or possessions, or position, or power?

What is it that's keeping you from returning this limitless love of Christ for you?

Is it worth it?

⨲

Jesus, I admit to being something like this wealthy young man. It's so hard to let go of the things that I think bring me security and fulfillment and joy. It's so hard to love you back with no fetters, no stumbling blocks, nothing to hold me back from following you with utter freedom and trust. I see you look at me with eyes of love, wanting me to come and follow you. Help me to keep my eyes locked on yours and not look back. Amen.

4. Reconciliation Comes First

> So when you are offering your gift at the altar,
> if you remember that your brother or sister has
> something against you, leave your gift there
> before the altar and go; first be reconciled to
> your brother or sister, and then come and offer
> your gift. —MATTHEW 5:23-24

From all appearances, it seemed as though another typical Sunday service was underway. The liturgy unfolded as usual. The scripture texts were read. And the gospel reading included Jesus's challenging words above.

The church where I worshiped that Sunday morning had had its share of in-house family struggles over recent years—perhaps more than its share. Yet somehow the members, representing both sides of a variety of hot-button issues, managed to come together around the table. Maybe grudgingly, but together.

But conflict would occasionally erupt, threatening the forced unity. Some hurtful words had been hurled. More than one back had been stabbed. And tensions simmered near the boiling point.

Just before the eucharist on this Sunday morning, the rector read this passage again. And decided to obey Jesus—to put the words into practice.

It was a definite risk. It could have gotten ugly. But he encouraged the people to meditate on the verses, to think about how they had hurt someone, and to go to that person and "make things right." Right now.

You could feel the congregation recoil at the thought. But the priest remained silent, coaxing them to meditate honestly, courageously, on Jesus's words.

Several minutes passed. Some coughs of discomfort, some shifting in the pews. Several more minutes passed.

Finally, a vestry member stood at his seat, looked across the sanctuary, and walked toward another vestry member. The look of surprise on the latter's face could be seen from across the sanctuary. The first man sat next to his fellow parishioner and spoke quietly, but firmly. Before long, the two men hugged, wiping tears from their eyes.

The congregation watched in awe as the scene unfolded. Then another member stood and walked to another member. Three more. Ten more. And in the next hour, amidst tears and hugs and warm conversations, two or three dozen folks made things right with each other.

Then, together, they broke the bread and drank the wine of the Lord's Supper.

No, this wasn't the end of conflict at the church. But what happened that Sunday morning did change things. Rarely were hot-button issues stifled and epithets muttered. Those who disagreed with each other made a much greater effort to talk things through because they valued the fact that, above all, they were siblings in Christ.

Following Jesus requires taking some difficult, risky, sometimes humiliating steps. But he beckons you to follow him to peace. Because reconciliation with one another comes first, even before coming to God in worship.

Are there people you know—family, friends, coworkers, neighbors, other church members—you need to reach out to? To talk things over with? To reconcile with? To make amends? To ask forgiveness? To forgive?

Is there something gnawing at you that keeps you from worshiping the Lord "in spirit and in truth"?

Put first things first. Accept the invitation. Take the initiative.

Then worship God together in peace.

Jesus, I acknowledge the need to be reconciled with some important people in my life. As I follow you and your example, give me the courage to take the first step, to reach out in love, humility, and forgiveness. Restore any broken relationships in the power of your Spirit. Amen.

Jesus Beckons You to Faith

5. Laughing at Jesus

> [Jesus] said, "Go away; for the girl is not dead
> but sleeping." And they laughed at him.
> —MATTHEW 9:24

"Go away."

That's more of an abrupt command than a gracious invitation. But sometimes Jesus must speak to us this way to grab our attention. To shock us into sense. To make us realize that our perception of our situation is precisely the opposite of the God-formed reality.

How often have you read something in the Bible and thought, "Ah, Jesus doesn't know what he's talking about." You might not admit that in public but deep down, you feel that way. You wonder: what is he asking me to believe here? What is he expecting that I, as his follower, should do?

What is he, nuts?

Those people gathered around Jairus's daughter certainly thought Jesus was being ridiculous. They even laughed at him. They were completely surprised by his nonsensical assertion. After all, the doctor had proclaimed her dead. Did he think they were crazy?

Even though we know the end of the story, can't we identify with them a little bit?

After all, we rationalize, Jesus doesn't understand our situation. Our world and culture are so different than when he walked the earth, we have to take those differences into account before we believe or do or say something ridiculous. People might talk. In fact, they might think *we're* nuts if we thought the way he thought or did what he encourages us to do. Right?

If Jairus had dismissed Jesus's words, he would have missed out on the miracle of his daughter's resurrection. And that makes me wonder:

How often do we miss out on the miracle Jesus has prepared to share with us?

How often do we walk away from a trying, tough situation, convinced it's hopeless, before inviting Jesus into it?

How often do we simply laugh at the big, bold proposition the Spirit brings to our heart because, well, it's impossible?

How strong is our faith—really?

Jesus says to you and me, "Go away."

To those of us who are grieving and mourning about what we would assume to be a lifeless tragedy, Jesus says, Your thinking is upside down and backwards. Your assumptions are what is dead here—dead wrong. Your understanding is faulty, colored by your own misperceptions, fears, and doubts. Your faith is empty and powerless because you're so busy mourning over what you think reality is that you miss the true reality—that God can break in and transform the situation. That God can bring life out of death.

"But when the crowd had been put outside, he went in and took her by the hand, and the girl got up" (Matthew 9:25).

If you want more faith, ask yourself:

What situations in my life would Jesus confront?

In what areas is my faith faulty, weak, or nonexistent?

What doubts are keeping me powerless?

What absurd prompting of the Spirit do I keep ignoring?

What false assumptions prevent me from experiencing God's powerful, surprising, and life-giving will?

Those are the things in our mind and heart to which we must say, "Go away." So that Jesus can come in, go to work, and surprise us.

Jesus, open my eyes to my doubt and unbelief in your power to transform. Let me see the areas of my relationship with you that you yearn to bring to life. And help me open myself fully to life-giving faith in you. Amen.

6. Be Clean

> A leper came to him begging him, and kneeling
> he said to him, "If you choose, you can make
> me clean." Moved with pity, Jesus stretched out
> his hand and touched him, and said to him, "I
> do choose. Be made clean!" Immediately the
> leprosy left him, and he was made clean.
> —MARK 1:40-42

People suffering with leprosy were outcasts in the Jewish
system. Their condition made them unacceptable in any social
activity, let alone worship. They were *personae non gratae*. They
had no champion, no protector.

Until Jesus arrives.

In the story, a bold leprous man approaches Jesus weakly on
his knees but strong in faith. Somehow he knows who Jesus
is. He has heard stories, perhaps even seen Jesus in action. He
doesn't even ask for healing, he simply states the truth: "If you
want to, you can cleanse me."

This man surely wants to be cleansed of his disease. And he knows he has come to the right person for it. But he also knows it is Jesus's decision to heal him.

The man's bold statement of faith pierces the heart of the Lord. Jesus breaks all sorts of religious laws and social graces by reaching out to the deformed man and touching him.

Then he speaks a glorious imperative to this hopeful soul: "Be made clean."

Immediately the words have their intended effect: The man is completely healed and whole.

In our society today, we don't have to deal with the discomfort of the presence of lepers. Medical science has virtually eliminated the disease, or at least controlled it as effectively as possible. In fact, scholars tell us the disease called leprosy in the Bible was probably unlike the disease we call leprosy today. We might hear of missions to lepers in some far-flung corner of the globe, but it's just not a problem in our culture today.

So, when we read accounts of people who suffered from leprosy approaching Jesus, we hardly feel the dread, the deep fear even, that this action would have elicited. At that time, our immediate response would have been to run away to protect ourselves.

Yet Jesus does not run. Rather, he reaches out in an act of total acceptance. His desire is that this faithful man be restored and renewed, and he has the power to accomplish that.

While we don't often run into people suffering with leprosy today, we do encounter folks we'd just as soon run away from: people from different countries, with different skin colors, of different faiths.; people whose sexual orientation or gender identity is different from ours; people with contagious diseases; people who are homeless.

But then, each of us is a leper in some sense. There are most likely things about us that other people would run away from in terror if they only knew. Perhaps we are suffering from rejection and avoidance, from shame and insecurity or some other barrier.

First, let's take our disease—and our dis-ease—to Jesus and have faith that if he wants to, he can cleanse us. And he wants to.

Then, let's turn around and accept by faith the loving invitation of Jesus to not run away from the "untouchables" of our society but rather to reach out and touch them with the loving and cleansing power of the Savior.

Jesus, thank you for wanting to heal me. Thank you for the example of reaching out to others who need a loving, healing touch. I feel your unflinching touch upon my festering wounds. Now, I want to follow you in reaching out to others. Amen.

7. Facing the Storm

He woke up and rebuked the wind, and said to
the sea, "Peace! Be still!" Then the wind ceased,
and there was a dead calm. He said to them,
"Why are you afraid? Have you still no faith?"
—Mark 4:39-40

❧

Years ago, a friend of mine from church invited me and
another fellow to spend a few hours relaxing on his brand-new
sailboat on Lake Lanier, north of Atlanta.

I knew nothing about sailing, but the other two did, so I just
went along for the ride. It was a peaceful, balmy summer's
eve. Several boats were out enjoying the gentle breezes wafting
around the glorious green hills that fell into the human-
made lake.

We sailed leisurely around the lake, chatting about current
events with each other, catching up on our lives. At one point,
the sails were adjusted and my friend the captain told me to tie
down a line. I did, to the best of my ability. As I said, I am not
a sailor. And I never did learn all those knots they taught us in
Cub Scouts.

In a matter of seconds, a summer thunderstorm descended forcefully upon us. A fierce wind caught our sails and tipped us precariously over—the mast was nearly parallel with the water surface.

We were about to sink.

My friend the captain shouted orders to the other "crewmember"—and I got out of the way. "We've got to lower the sails! Loose that line!" he ordered. The other man tried desperately to obey—but my knot was a good old square knot rather than the slip knot that should have immediately pulled loose with one tug.

"It's knotted up—I can't untie it!" he yelled to the captain.

"If you don't untie it, we'll sink!" the captain yelled, in command yet nevertheless panicking.

The realization hit me with the force of the sudden summer storm: my stupid knot was about to sink his brand-new sailboat… and we could all drown.

Thanks be to God, just before we all got tossed into the lake, my shipmate got that stubborn knot of mine loose. The captain frantically pulled down the sail so the wind had nothing to grab on to, and the ship began to right itself.

We motored to the dock, the three of us sweating and breathing heavily.

I wonder what we would have done if Jesus had been on board with us. Would we have been so panicky? After all, the disciples were.

For Jesus, it had been a long, hard day of teaching and ministering to the growing crowds following him, clamoring for him, needing him. When evening came, he wanted to get away, go to the other side of the sea away from Galilee to the area of the Gerasenes. So, he called his disciples into the boat and sailed away. Of course, he couldn't really escape: Several other boats followed him.

Jesus, the Son of God, was tired. He crawled into the stern of the boat and fell fast asleep. It was evidently a very sound sleep.

"A great gale arose, and the waves beat into the boat, so that the boat was already being swamped. But he was in the stern, asleep on the cushion; and they woke him up and said to him, 'Teacher, do you not care that we are perishing?'"
(Mark 4:37-38).

Have you ever been awakened from a deep sleep by an excited, frightened, panicked person? Maybe a child afraid of the thunder and lightning? Or an emergency phone call? Or a spouse upset after a nightmare?

If so, you know that when you're tired and resting deeply, the last thing you want is somebody demanding your immediate attention and accusing you of indifference, of not caring.

But Jesus's panicking disciples roused him. His first words were directed to the raging storm: "Peace! Be still!" Of course, he might also have aimed those words at his faithless followers, as if telling frightened children to settle down and be quiet.

The miracle of his authority over nature must have left them stunned and slack jawed. His reprimand doubtless made them feel small; it's clear he was telling them that they, too, could exercise this same sort of power if they only had faith.

Lest we be too critical of the disciples, let's admit that we are much like them. When one of life's storms—illness, job loss, betrayal, stress—overwhelms us, we often panic. Instead of confronting the situation in the power and wisdom of God almighty, we run around screaming in terror. Hopeless. Certain we're about to drown. Yelling to the Lord to help us. Because he doesn't even seem to notice the horrible problems we're facing.

Why are we such cowards? Why do we not believe what Jesus tells us? Why is our faith so small?

Jesus tells us—and the storms around us— "Peace! Be still!"

The next time you find yourself in the middle of a sudden storm, trust the One who can command the storm to cease.

❧

Jesus, I can identify with the disciples. At the first sign of trouble, I want to run away. I scream at you, angry that you don't seem to care. But I hear your invitation to be quiet, to trust, to exercise mature faith. Give me the strength and wisdom to accept that invitation, knowing that when the next storm hits, you are with me, and you empower me to overcome. Amen.

8. Why Cry?

> When the Lord saw her, he had compassion for
> her and said to her, "Do not weep." —LUKE 7:13

❧

Picture this: Jesus, surrounded by his twelve disciples and a
large crowd trailing behind them, walks into the village
of Nain. The atmosphere hums with joyful anticipation. The
word about this revolutionary preacher and healer has been
spreading like crabgrass on a summer lawn, and people are
coming from all around to catch the show.

It's a parade without the marching bands. The crowd
is chattering, wondering what will happen next. What
astonishing miracle will Jesus produce? What surprising truth
will he reveal? What challenging risk will he encourage his
followers to take?

On they walk, aged and young, men and women, believers
and skeptics. As they approach the village gates, this jubilant
crowd runs right into another parade of a much different sort:
a funeral procession. A hush falls on the boisterous followers.

A weeping mother leads a solemn line of mourners
surrounding a body. She has lost her son, and as a widow,

she is now completely alone, facing a life of emptiness and poverty in every sense of the word. As soon as Jesus sees the woman, his heart breaks. He knows the devastation she faces. Her loss is immeasurable. She has no husband, no son to provide for her in a culture that does little to provide for widows. His imperative to her elicits a gasp from both crowds: "Do not weep."

Don't cry? How can he say that? If anyone has a right to cry, it is this woman. She faces destitution and loneliness—and there is no way out. Except with Jesus.

Just then he does something that stuns the gathered witnesses: "Then he came forward and touched the bier, and the bearers stood still. And he said, 'Young man, I say to you, rise!'" (Luke 7:14).

Rise? How can the dead rise up?

First, Jesus tells the woman to stop crying, then he gives her the reason why: "The dead man sat up and began to speak, and Jesus gave him to his mother" (Luke 7:15).

In an instant, her life situation is utterly changed, her hope restored. She is saved through the miraculous act of this stranger leading a lively parade of motley followers.

Can you imagine being part of that parade? Seeing a miracle unfold before you so spontaneously, so powerfully? How would you respond?

The gospel story tells us how the crowd reacts: "Fear seized all of them; and they glorified God, saying, 'A great prophet has risen among us!' and 'God has looked favorably on his people!'" (Luke 7:16).

Suddenly, both sets of marchers—the curious and the mournful—are celebrating. The reality of what they had seen hits them like a nuclear blast at the core of their soul. They acknowledge the source of Christ's power and worship the holy mystery of God at work in their very presence. And they celebrate. Boisterously. Gratefully.

Put yourself in the place of the mourning mother. You like her have suffered a loss—a job, a friend, a spouse, a child, a dream. You feel unable to deal with the situation, empty of power and facing a hopeless future. And Jesus sees you. Jesus tells you, "Don't cry." Then Jesus gives you a reason not to weep.

Will you join the celebration of the faithful? Will you agree with the grateful, worshipful, noisy revelers that "God has looked favorably on his people"?

It's true. Believe it. This is where abundant life begins.

⊂∞⊃

Jesus, thank you for your revolutionary comfort. I celebrate your powerful care in my life. Thank you for seeing me, knowing me, loving me, accepting me. Help me do the same to others. Amen.

Jesus Beckons You to Love

9. Living with No Regrets

> Love your enemies, do good, and lend,
> expecting nothing in return. Your reward will
> be great, and you will be children of the Most
> High; for he is kind to the ungrateful and the
> wicked. Be merciful, just as your Father is
> merciful. —LUKE 6:35-36

Jesus holds out to us all a different way to live. This is a way of life that is, frankly, not natural for human beings, a way of life that goes against every typical human, self-protective, self-promoting thought and action, a way of life only God's Spirit can help us live, a way of life that is everlastingly rewarding.

It is the way of love.

It seems incomprehensible. Love your *enemies*? Give without expecting anything in return? Yet, this is the way God created us to live.

Jesus invites us to live into our God-given identity in the same way God the heavenly parent deals with us: mercifully, generously, graciously, lovingly.

We think we have nothing to give, and yet when we purposefully decide to live this way, we find limitless resources available to make it happen. But all too often, we're so afraid of failing at it that we don't even try.

Many years ago, I was talking with a friend about the pet dog I had at the time. He was a sweet, well-trained, handsome sharpei/lab mix, but he had more than enough aggravating habits to drive me to distraction at times. Over the years, he'd become increasingly frightened of thunderstorms, so even when it threatened to gently shower, he'd go berserk, chewing and scratching up doorways and walls in an effort to hide or escape. Wouldn't life be so much simpler without him, I thought?

But my friend told me about a dog he'd had for many years: a gray terrier mutt named John that his kids had brought home one day. After his kids moved out, he waited patiently for years for John to die a natural death. John stubbornly held on for fifteen years, driving him absolutely nuts at times with his frustrating canine habits.

Time after time after time, John would chew through the pickets of their backyard fence and escape. My friend would conceive new ways to block his access to the fence, but John would always find a way around them—resulting in numerous tickets from animal control. One day, the police showed up at my friend's professional office threatening to take him to jail for "contempt of court." Apparently one of the animal control citations issued when John had rampaged through the neighborhood had inadvertently gone unpaid.

It would have been so easy to choose to get rid of that dog, he told me. "But John taught me a lot about loving. After all, love is a choice, and I made the conscious decision to love John. I learned how to put up with his bad habits and appreciate his loyal love for me. And before long, I was applying this concept of deciding to love to other people, including myself. John changed my life."

Love is a choice. It's a hard choice. It's messy and painful and comes with all sorts of ramifications and reactions and difficult situations in its wake.

But God chooses to love us.

No matter what, God always chooses to love us. And there is no changing the divine mind. We're messy. We keep trying to escape. We struggle against that love because it makes no sense to us.

Nevertheless, God loves us mercifully, forever.

That's nice, but it doesn't stop there. Jesus calls us to love others in this same way—and not just annoying pets, but everyone. We're to love the neighbors we just can't seem to get along with. Co-workers who keep stabbing us in the back with our superiors. People who believe or vote differently from us. People whose orientation or gender identity make us uncomfortable. Sick people. Imprisoned people. Contagious people.

Just people. Just everyone.

Think how kind and merciful God has been with you. Think what God has put up with from you over the years. Yet God is merciful.

You be merciful, too.

❧

Jesus, you make it sound so easy. Just love people. Why is this decision so difficult to make? What keeps me from sticking my neck out to help others? What am I afraid of? Help me appreciate all the kindness and mercy God so abundantly shows me, so that I can be empowered to show others kindness and mercy—generously and graciously. In the power of the Spirit, Amen.

10. *Giving, Not Getting*

> Do not judge, and you will not be judged; do
> not condemn, and you will not be condemned.
> Forgive, and you will be forgiven; give, and it
> will be given to you. A good measure, pressed
> down, shaken together, running over, will be
> put into your lap; for the measure you give will
> be the measure you get back. —LUKE 6:37-38

Life is full of conditions. Just look at an ad for an automobile lease or cell phone plan, and you'll see line after line of indecipherable fine print. Or try to understand a simple contract for purchasing a home—do lawyers even understand all that it says? Or read a news story about some celebrity couple's extensive prenuptial agreement. I dare you.

Now meditate on Eugene Peterson's version of this passage from *The Message*:

> Don't pick on people, jump on their failures, criticize
> their faults—unless, of course, you want the same
> treatment. Don't condemn those who are down; that
> hardness can boomerang. Be easy on people; you'll
> find life a lot easier. Give away your life; you'll find life

given back, but not merely given back—given back with bonus and blessing. Giving, not getting, is the way. Generosity begets generosity.

Now consider your own relationships.

Be honest—we place all sorts of conditions on others we're in relationship with, from our closest family members to those we simply pass on the street. If we get enough from these people, then we'll give to them. If they pay us enough attention or give us the right compliments, then we'll be nice to them. If they don't bother us too much, then we won't bother them. On and on the conditions go, so many ifs and thens.

Jesus beckons us into another way: the way of unconditional love. Giving generously to others without expecting anything back, without judging them by their appearance or their situation, without any secret motives or hidden agenda. Just giving. Just loving.

According to Jesus, that means not finding fault with others, picking on their inadequacies, or shoving their failures in their faces. When we treat others that way, we open the door to the exact same treatment. Do we really want that?

Condemning those who are "beneath you," feeling just a little better than others, only builds hardness on your heart—a hardness that can ricochet right back in your face.

"Be easy on people; you'll find life a lot easier."

Isn't that true? You know that feeling that erupts when you're rushed and overwhelmed by various responsibilities and someone interrupts with a matter that needs your immediate attention? It's easy to bite off the person's head. But you also know how much fun it is to be easy, to crack a joke, to ask how the person is doing. Everybody wins.

You hear a lot about karma—what goes around comes around. What you do, for good or ill, will come back to you.

Jesus preaches the same truth: "Give away your life; you'll find life given back." That's how it works in this universe of God's. But that's not all: Jesus says the life you experience when you live generously is "not merely given back—[but] given back with bonus and blessing."

Doesn't that sound like the kind of life you've been waiting to experience? That you've been yearning for God to give you?

It all starts with a decision to love others unconditionally.

❧

Jesus, I've been conditioned to look out for myself, to figure out how I can get what I want at whatever cost necessary. Cleanse me of my selfish drive—help me channel that drive outward rather than inward, so that I can be a channel of your unconditional, selfless, giving love to anyone I meet today. Amen.

11. Love and Let Love

> Why do you see the speck in your neighbor's
> eye, but do not notice the log in your own eye?
> Or how can you say to your neighbor, 'Friend,
> let me take out the speck in your eye,' when
> you yourself do not see the log in your own
> eye? You hypocrite, first take the log out of your
> own eye, and then you will see clearly to take
> the speck out of your neighbor's eye.
> —LUKE 6:41-42

Woven throughout Jesus's words in the gospels is a common theme: don't judge other people. Consider carefully instead your life, your relationship with God, and leave everyone else to God.

But look around the church today, or take a trip through church history, and you'll see this is one of the most frequently ignored or broken commands Jesus gave us.

Why do we insist that our way is always the "right" way? Why do we feel the need to be better than others who don't look or believe or dress or live the way we think they should?

It's not a question of who's right and who's wrong. We can't all be right. The thing is, it doesn't matter. If we focus on our own faults and inadequacies instead of others', we'll find plenty of flaws that need addressing.

I found myself struggling with this word of Jesus some time ago when attending a religious media convention and representing the *Day 1* ministry. Frankly, I didn't believe the same way many of the folks attending this convention believed as they were typically deeply conservative, religiously and politically. Sometimes hearing them talk made my skin crawl. I was in such a furor of self-righteous judgmentalism that I could hardly stand to be in the same gigantic convention hall with some of them for too long. I felt like I was about to explode.

The second day of the convention I was wandering around the exhibit hall, clucking my tongue at some of the displays that seemed especially over the top. Then, surprisingly, I came upon a booth with two acquaintances who represented another religious organization I had worked with for years. I knew we were of the same stripe.

The three of us nearly jumped for joy seeing others of our own kind. Immediately, we started jabbering back and forth, "Can you believe what that speaker said?" and "Did you see those outrageous bumper stickers at that booth up the aisle here?" and "Oh, it's so good to see someone we can be ourselves with!"

The irony is, I'm sure several folks at that convention could have said the very same things about us.

Later, of course, God set my thinking a little straighter as I met more and more wonderful, thoughtful Christian people at this convention and found them to be utterly charming and guileless.

Sure, there are stubborn, hardheaded people on all sides of every issue. Jesus invites us to live differently, to stop worrying about the little specks in their eyes when we are carrying our own woodpile of issues.

I've been amazed to discover that many of the people I have disagreed with for so long have turned out to be some of the most genuine, caring people I have known. Not that I'm judging, you understand. But it's so easy to fall into kneejerk reactions to any issue that we never get around to discovering this delightful fact.

Jesus invites us to live and let live. And to love and let love.

❦

Jesus, it's so much easier to see others' faults. To consider my own, I must take the initiative to study the mirror—the mirror of God's word, the mirror of the Spirit's presence—to see the areas of my own life that need serious attention. Help me to look upward for your help and inward at my needs, rather than outward at everyone else's shortcomings. Keep me from being judgmental, for your sake. Amen.

12. How to Go All In

> [The man] answered, "You shall love the Lord
> your God with all your heart, and with all your
> soul, and with all your strength, and with all
> your mind; and your neighbor as yourself."
> And [Jesus] said to him, "You have given the
> right answer; do this, and you will live."
> —LUKE 10:27-28

I've always been intrigued by Scotland because William
Wallace is a national hero—and we share the same clan
surname. Surely, I am a descendant—even though he had no
known children.

My family always claimed Scotland as our homeland; only
later did I learn I had a Scots ancestor named Peter Wallace
who sailed to America in the eighteenth century. Somewhat
serendipitous, I think, even though I was named for the
apostle.

I was fortunate to take a dream trip to Scotland in 1997,
not long after the motion picture *Braveheart* was released.
That film recounted (in typical Hollywood hyperbole) the
legend of William Wallace, and as a result, the whole country

of Scotland had gone Wallace-crazy with creative museum presentations and special events.

As a Wallace myself, I was thrilled to say the least. When that September travel day arrived, I could hardly contain myself. My trans-Atlantic flight was, thankfully, uneventful (even though I was surrounded in coach by a famous dance troupe). After a brief stopover in Paris, the flight arrived in Edinburgh, albeit without my luggage, which was, thankfully, delivered soon to our charming hotel.

Though I had slept poorly if at all on the flight over, I hit the Scottish ground running. After checking in at the hotel, I immediately set off on foot toward Edinburgh's City Center, taking it all in.

My mouth was agape. That entire week, as I traveled from Edinburgh's Royal Mile to St. Andrews to Stirling to Crail to the Trossachs to Caithness and elsewhere, I simply couldn't get enough of the sights and sounds (yes, there are bagpipes in Scotland) and smells and tastes (yes, even haggis). I breathed it all in. I wanted every moment to last an hour, I wanted to grab every memory and hold on to it forever.

I don't think I had ever been more engaged and energized in my life. Everything seemed realer than real. Going all in for the experience, I felt vibrant, expectant, full of life.

When I returned home, it was back to reality. I eventually receded back into my protective shell of routine busyness. But I wondered, why can't I live this passionately all the time?

Why can't I approach my relationship with God with all my heart, and with all my soul, and with all my strength, and with all my mind—the way I approached each day's touring in Scotland? Why can't I relate to my world, my family, my work, my ministry, with all that fresh enthusiasm and interaction?

And, by the way, why can't you?

I have tried to live this way in all I do: going all in, giving my whole heart/soul/strength/mind for God. That was my approach several years ago during the year-long discernment I undertook to become a postulant for the priesthood, taking every encounter that came along and jumping all in. It changed my life.

A religious scholar asked Jesus what he had to do to live eternally. At Jesus's prompting, he summarized God's Law simply: Love God with everything you have, and love your neighbor as you do yourself.

It was the correct answer. Only one more thing, Jesus said: "Do this, and you will live."

Do it. Just do it today: live and love God passionately with all that you are, all that God created you to be.

Jesus, I want to love with everything I've got. I want to live. Fully. Completely. All in. With nothing holding me back. I want to be yours wholly, unstoppably. Please show me how. Amen.

13. Turning Back to Love

> Remember then from what you have fallen;
> repent, and do the works you did at first. If
> not, I will come to you and remove your
> lampstand from its place, unless you repent.
> —REVELATION 2:5

If Jesus were to speak to me, I hope he would say positive, encouraging things. Tell me what a great job I'm doing. Acknowledge all the hard work I've put in on his behalf. Just, you know, be nice to me.

After all, he says such things to the church at Ephesus. He tells the apostle to send a letter to the church with these words: "I know your works, your toil and your patient endurance. I know that you cannot tolerate evildoers; you have tested those who claim to be apostles but are not, and have found them to be false. I also know that you are enduring patiently and bearing up for the sake of my name, and that you have not grown weary" (Revelation 2:2-3).

Isn't that encouraging? Jesus tells the believers there that he knows them, watches over them as they seek to serve him. He sees their efforts, their hard work, their refusal to quit, their courage for the cause.

Maybe he knows us too, watches over us and sees what we're up to. So, what would Jesus tell us if he dictated a letter to us? Would he compliment us on our endurance, our commitment, our dedication to truth and justice? Would he applaud our undaunted courage in the face of opposition?

It's clear the believers at Ephesus are working diligently together for the faith. They stand firmly for Christ, especially against those who promote false and untrustworthy teachings.

If you heard those words from your Lord, you'd want to let them soak in. Unfortunately for the church at Ephesus, Jesus has a "but" for them:"But I have this against you, that you have abandoned the love you had at first" (Revelation 2:4).

Ouch.

Yes, they may be doing all the right things, but apparently they are doing them for the wrong reasons, in the wrong power. They have lost their first love. They may be doctrinally pure and argue the fine points of the truth well. But they aren't acting out of the generative love of Christ, the love that wooed them into the fold in the first place.

Their goal has become proving themselves right, overcoming views they consider wrong and harmful. They have lost sight of the main reason Jesus had come: to invite people into loving relationship with God, to love God with heart and soul and strength and mind, and their neighbors—all of them—as themselves.

I don't know about you, but Jesus's words make me uncomfortable. Because like the Ephesians, I can point to all the right things I'm doing, but I realize with a stab to my heart that I do many of those things out of self-promoting, self-protecting motivations.

So many times, it feels like I, too, have fallen away from my first love.

Have you?

Happily, Jesus provides the Ephesians—and you and me—a way to reclaim that first love, to let it rejuvenate our work and refresh our motivations: "Repent, and do the works you did at first."

It's a wake-up call to turn back around, to purposefully reclaim the deep, meaningful, early love that filled us to overflowing when we first met Jesus. He urges us to recall that energizing, effervescent grace and acceptance of others and reach out to them in the spirit of Christ no matter who they were or what they believed or what their life situation may be, and invite them into the loving family knit together in and by Jesus's sacrificial love.

Maybe you've experienced this turning back. I have, multiple times. I am so grateful that, every time, Jesus welcomes me back.

One such time for me came many years ago, after I'd worked several years in a religious organization. After those years of hard work, I reached the burnout point. I began doubting, questioning. On top of that, I was facing lonely struggles in my personal life that made me question God's very existence.

Slowly, with the help of some mentors, my soul began turning around, starting over afresh. As a result, it seemed my priorities changed radically. My relationship with God seemed renewed, more real and authentic. I wasn't simply going through the motions of being a "good Christian." I was instead seeking God for strength and guidance and letting that work through me.

Even with this deeper relationship, I find I continually need to hear Jesus's word to me: *Turn back around, renew your relationship with me.*

Put yourself in the Ephesian church in the early days. Listen for Jesus's clear and loving challenge. Reconsider your motives. And recover your dear early love for him.

Jesus, it's so easy for me to get caught up in the responsibilities of following you faithfully and start fulfilling them in the wrong spirit, in my own power and wisdom. Please remind me to turn back when I have gone too far in the wrong direction. Thank you for beckoning me back to the early love you and I shared and for encouraging me to live out of that love in the present. Amen.

Jesus Beckons You to Serve

14. Golden Advice

> In everything do to others as you would have
> them do to you; for this is the law and the
> prophets. —Matthew 7:12

Decades after my first encounters with them, a couple of my childhood heroes continued to lift my spirit and entertain my soul. These two people contributed, at least in some small way, to forming my belief system and maybe even some aspects of my personality.

Who are they? Soupy Sales and Stan Lee.

Surprised? I'm serious.

Stan Lee, as you may know, was the co-creator of such beloved comic-book characters as Spider-man, Hulk, Fantastic Four, Thor, and Daredevil (all of which, and many others, have been featured in major motion pictures in recent years).

As a kid, I was enamored with Lee's comic-books tales of derring-do and do-gooding. Like most preadolescents, I especially identified with born loser and nerdy teenager Peter Parker, who, bitten by a radioactive spider while fighting acne, donned homemade blue-and-red spider-webbed tights to prosecute justice and protect humankind from all sorts of evildoers.

Why? Peter's late Uncle Ben taught him that "with great power comes great responsibility." In other words, we've all been given powerful gifts, and we should use them for the good of others.

At the same time, the comedian Soupy Sales was one of my childhood idols because I found him hilarious. What's more, he was from my hometown of Huntington, West Virginia—a local guy who made good. I attended the same high school and college Soupy did.

When his New York-based daily children's program aired regularly, I would make a beeline home from school to catch it and laugh myself silly watching White Fang and Black Tooth, the wacky door-to-door salesmen, and so many other characters interact with Soupy, who always seemed to let us in on the gag with a warm wink and a big smile.

Some years ago, after I had long become an adult (in body if not mind), my two heroes seemed to collude to make me think seriously about something. I was fortunate to meet and correspond with Stan Lee for the last two decades of his life, and he was always most gracious and encouraging with me—as he was with everyone, it seemed.

After I sent him a copy of a devotional book I wrote on the life and ministry of Christ, Stan emailed back a hearty thank you. And he added: "In your card you wrote, 'Our faiths may differ, but….' I beg to disagree. I think our *faiths* are similar—it's merely our religions that may differ…. I have the greatest respect for any discipline that preaches kindness and charity and love for one's fellow man. Most important of all, to me, 'Do unto others as you'd have them do unto you' is the greatest phrase ever written. If everyone followed that creed, this world would be a paradise."

The very next day, I happened to be reading Soupy Sales's autobiography, *Soupy Sez! My Life and Zany Times*, and stumbled upon this passage: "Throughout my career, I've tried to be as generous and kind as I possibly could to everyone. In fact—I know this sounds corny—but it's the truth; my motto is, was, and always will be, 'Do unto others as you would have them do unto you.'"

Reading that well-known Golden Rule twice in two days from two childhood heroes had an impact on me as an adult. Both had been "good" guys in every sense of the word over the years, and now I understood why.

I know the quotation well: Jesus, in his Sermon on the Mount, offers the summary of the scriptures. The NRSV puts it: "In everything do to others as you would have them do to you." But I love how Eugene Peterson has crafted it in *The Message*: "Ask yourself what you want people to do for you, then grab the initiative and do it for them."

Of course, just about every religion on earth reflects this concept. But few people have exemplified the Golden Rule as Jesus himself did.

The Golden Rule is not about our expectations regarding how others are supposed to treat *us*—or about waiting to see how *we're* treated before we do anything. It has nothing to do with "an eye for an eye" or "what goes around comes around."

Rather, the Golden Rule starts with each of us taking proactive steps to serve others, to treat them as we'd like to be treated. It's taking the responsibility to do good for others regardless of what they do for us.

What if we actually put the Golden Rule to work in our lives? What if we looked for opportunities to serve others with kindness and self-sacrifice? What if we went out of our way to do something positive and helpful for someone in need?

Of course, none of us real human beings have super powers. But if we put into practice even the most basic elements of faith, particularly with a sense of humor and goodwill, we can experience a bit of paradise on this cold, hard earth.

It's within our power. And remember, with great power comes great responsibility.

❧

Jesus, it's simple, really, isn't it? Treat others like I want to be treated. And do it first. Help me take on that simple, though seemingly insurmountable, task. Just for today. And maybe again tomorrow. Amen.

15. For the Glory

> Beware of practicing your piety before others
> in order to be seen by them; for then you have
> no reward from your Father in heaven.
> —MATTHEW 6:1

Just when we are about to pat ourselves on the back for our good deeds, Jesus invites us to question our motives.

We already know we're supposed to serve others, to help those on society's margins, to provide our time, our resources, and our abilities for the cause of Christ. But Jesus wants us to take our act a step further and consider why we do what we do.

Are we performing so others can see what wonderful Christians we are?

Are we hopeful that our boss sees us taking extra time, making extra effort, so that when it's time to be considered for a pay raise, she might be better inclined to reward us?

Are we hoping to impress that special somebody—the boyfriend or girlfriend, the important leader, the colleague, the spouse, the pastor, the neighbor, whoever it might be—with our magnificent goodness?

How marvelous we are! See how helpful we can be? Be amazed at what brilliant servants we are! Watch how we share the love of Christ with others in need.

I have a confession: I deeply hope others notice my good deeds and how many extra hours I put in at work. I desperately want others to see me and be positively impressed by what a great guy I am—with the hope that they will like me more or pay me more or treat me even better.

Churches and organizations today have been well trained by the corporate world to announce any positive step they take or good news that might come their way by issuing a press release or a TikTok or YouTube video or a social media burst. They promote the "good news" anywhere they can, so people will realize what good people they are, what dedicated Christians, working so hard for God.

Before the transaction was touchscreen automated, I always wanted to make sure the barista at Starbucks noticed I left my extra change in the tip jar. I hated it when they looked away just as I was dropping in that beat-up buck. I even thought of reaching in and pulling it back out to make sure they saw me drop it in—but I feared they'd think I was stealing.

Jesus calls us out on this kind of self-centered, self-promoting behavior. He wants our motives to be pure and honest, God-centered and God-promoting. He beckons us to serve God, to do what's right. To fulfill the call of justice. To sacrifice and deny ourselves. To go the extra mile.

All for God's sake. Not ours.

And to do it as privately and discreetly as we possibly can.

Jesus adds: "When you do something for someone else, don't call attention to yourself. You've seen them in action, I'm sure— 'playactors' I call them—treating prayer meeting and street corner alike as a stage, acting compassionate as long as someone is watching, playing to the crowds. They get applause, true, but that's all they get" (Matthew 6:2, *The Message*).

Jesus invites us to do good things for the glory. Not ours. God's.

Jesus, give me insight into my motives. Through your Spirit within me, make me aware of times I'm doing this for my glory rather than yours. I want to serve you with a clean heart—not a double mind. Amen.

16. The Most Valuable Treasure

> Do not store up for yourselves treasures on
> earth, where moth and rust consume and
> where thieves break in and steal; but store up
> for yourselves treasures in heaven, where
> neither moth nor rust consumes and where
> thieves do not break in and steal. For where
> your treasure is, there your heart will be also.
> —Matthew 6:19-21

❦

I confess to being a hoarder. I don't typically hoard items of
value to anyone else (no, I have no hidden safe filled with rare
gems, no personal galleries of original Van Goghs or Monets,
although I do have moldering in my closet a box or two of
comic books that may or may not be worth a few bucks).
No, the things I hoard are valuable pretty much only to me.
They are personal treasures. Boxes of old magazines, copies
of newspapers I had a hand in producing, school papers and
other memorabilia from elementary through college, journal
upon journal, pocket calendars, mementos from various trips
and vacations, and scads of letters from family members,
old buddies.

But I am a *recovering* hoarder. My spouse has encouraged me in recent years to practice this verse from Matthew when it comes to earthly treasures. And more and more, I realize that I really don't need most of this stuff; I never even look at it.

And, in many cases, time's effects have made some of them nearly useless. Pages are yellowing and brittle, even bug eaten. I was deeply disappointed some years ago to discover that my junior high yearbooks—one of which I helped put together, including the cover design—had gotten damp and mildewed and wrinkled and all the pages stuck together.

So why do I hold on to those things? I guess I want to hold on to the pleasant memories they rekindle—the friends and loved ones, the personal accomplishments, the memorable events, the special places. All these things have meaning for me, and I fear I will lose that meaning if I don't have something concrete to prove that I once had it.

Many years ago, I read an article about scientific studies of the brain in which an electric stimulus was applied to various parts of a subject's brain. When the electricity flowed, a memory stored in that area of the brain was replayed almost like a 3-D movie in the subject's mind—the sounds, smells, and feelings all came back as the scene replayed itself.

I often wonder what that would be like, reliving a memory stored in my brain on command. It's appealing to me in some odd way—like watching high-tech home movies. Of course,

I'd only want to relive the pleasant and joyful memories, and it's not like my brain cells are cataloged in file folders.

But do I really want to relive my life? Or do I want to live my life now and build new memories for the future—and for eternity?

By holding on to such existential ephemera, I am in a sense forcing myself to look backward, to keep my mind and my heart in the past. This tendency can keep me from being in the present, from being *with* those around me *now* where rich reality resides. And it can keep me from looking forward to the future and living in a way that leads me in a positive direction.

I don't think there's anything wrong with keeping mementos of a life enjoyably lived. But there is something wrong when we need those things to feel good about ourselves, when we hold onto them to feel as though we have a life, when in reality our life is happening right now and just ahead of us.

Jesus invites us to "store up... treasures in heaven" because "where your treasure is, there your heart will be also."

How do we stockpile treasure in heaven? As Christians, we know it's spiritually counterproductive to stockpile valuables here on earth—cars and houses and jewels and buildings and stocks and all that—although few of us really get a good grip on what that means in this consumerist culture of ours.

But what's the alternative? Clearly, a life of service to others in Jesus's name, a life well lived in God's eyes, will be rewarded in heaven in some way that will blow our puny human minds.

If we were to take Jesus seriously about his admonitions to reach out to the sick and the prisoners and the naked and the hungry, I suppose we would find out more fully what he means by "treasures in heaven."

In the meantime, we need to ask ourselves: "Where do we most want to be? Lost in a past we cannot relive or change? Or creating a life in the *now*—a servant's life that will help us prepare the way for an eternity with God that forever celebrates a life well lived?"

Excuse me, but I have a closet to clean out.

⌘

Jesus, help me to refocus my attention on the treasures of heaven instead of the silly, useless, and outdated ephemera of this life. Give me the insight, the strength, and the boldness to make generous deposits to my heavenly stockpile today. Amen.

17. Set Free to Serve

> Therefore I tell you, do not worry about
> your life, what you will eat or what you
> will drink, or about your body, what you will
> wear. Is not life more than food, and the body
> more than clothing? Look at the birds of the
> air; they neither sow nor reap nor gather into
> barns, and yet your heavenly Father feeds
> them. Are you not of more value than they?
> —MATTHEW 6:25-26

❦

Our consumer-oriented culture saturates us with messages about what we should look like, dress like, eat like, feel like, be like. Should we purchase name-brand clothing or check out the sales at the off-price online store? Meanwhile, in other parts of the world, our siblings are wondering where their next meal is coming from.

To all of us around the world, Jesus makes a shocking invitation.

In essence, he's saying: *Don't worry. God will take care of you. While you're burning up so much time and energy fretting about the things of life, you're avoiding the real issues.*

"Is not life more than food, and the body more than clothing?" Jesus asks us. If you have decided to follow the way of Jesus, then get your priorities straight.

What are those priorities?

✤ Worshiping God

✤ Serving others who don't have the food or clothing they need

✤ Reaching out to someone in deep emotional distress with words of comfort, hope, and understanding or simply listening to them with open hearts

✤ Helping meet the needs of those who can't care for themselves because of illness or physical challenges

✤ Speaking truth to power, encouraging those in authority to open their eyes and hearts to unmet needs and injustices in your community

✤ Visiting those in prison

✤ Providing for widows and orphans, or others suffering from immense loss

✚ Offering the bread of life to someone whose life seems out of control and hopeless

✚ Living a life marked by justice, mercy, and humility

The list could go on and on, but just think what you could do with all these priorities if you would trust Jesus to meet all your needs—if you were set free to serve in Jesus's name. It's just basic Christianity.

Jesus beckons you to look at the birds of the air. Free. Unfettered. Trusting. Careless in God's care.

Wouldn't you like to live that way? To experience that carelessness in your soul? To be able to share a foolishly lavish love and care for others in need around you? To experience unfettered, unrestricted freedom from worry, from the myriad details of making your life appear as acceptable to others as possible?

Look at the birds. God takes care of them, giving them everything they need to be free birds. And you are worth so much more to God than those birds.

God yearns that you, like those birds, would let go of the anxiety that keeps you from being all God created you to be.

And fly.

Jesus, I confess I get all tied up in my concerns about life here and now. Help me to reset my priorities, to clear out my muddled, self-consumed mind, and to love and serve lavishly today. Amen.

18. The Face of Jesus

Then the king will say to those at his right
hand, "Come, you that are blessed by my
Father, inherit the kingdom prepared for you
from the foundation of the world; for I was
hungry and you gave me food, I was thirsty
and you gave me something to drink, I was a
stranger and you welcomed me, I was naked
and you gave me clothing, I was sick and you
took care of me, I was in prison and you visited
me." —MATTHEW 25:34-36

❧

Jesus tells a story about two kinds of people. He calls them
"sheep" and "goats." They have very different purposes in life.
The goats are self-centered, oblivious to the needs of others,
striving only to care for themselves. The sheep are precisely
the opposite.

In the story, Jesus explains that at some point these two groups
will be separated forever. Until then, they will live together,
work together, play together—at home, at work, at church,
in the community. But at some point, the distinction must
be made, and the ramifications of their life choices will be
manifest.

Only the sheep will hear the precious invitation from Jesus to "come." Only the sheep will be able to enjoy eternal communion with God. Only the sheep will get what's coming to them in the kingdom of heaven.

And why? What have they done to deserve this?

Well, of course, they have done nothing. We don't work our way into heaven. Christ has provided the way of love himself.

But strangely, Jesus doesn't explain this to the disciples. He doesn't set forth a clear presentation of the gospel to ensure that his listeners understand the "steps necessary for salvation." Wouldn't this have been an ideal time to do so?

Instead, Jesus sets out clear and even surprising reasons as to why the sheep get to spend eternity in communal bliss:

> They fed the hungry.

> They brought water to the thirsty.

> They provided shelter for the homeless.

> They gave clothes to those who had none.

> They visited the sick.

> They ministered to those in prison.

To the "goats" who argue about this division, Jesus explains, "I'm telling the solemn truth: Whenever you did one of these things to someone overlooked or ignored, that was me—you did it to me" (*The Message,* Matthew 25:40).

This is where I really start feeling uncomfortable. How about you?

Frankly, I haven't done a whole lot of feeding the hungry or visiting the prisoners. Oh, I've done a few things—spent the night in a homeless shelter, once. Served in a church soup kitchen a few times. Gave my used clothes to the Cathedral Thrift Store—unless I could sell them at a garage sale.

Yet Jesus uses these descriptions to explain who will be invited into the realm of God forever.

Is he saying that these sorts of self-sacrificial acts—not unlike his own on the cross—are representative of those whose lives have truly been touched by his healing power and grace? Is he saying that those who truly know Jesus and follow his way of love will be involved, not only in sharing the words of good news but also in sharing the deeds of service to those who need hope and mercy?

Is he saying that the redeemed—those whose lives have been touched and cleansed and changed and empowered by God—naturally seek to reach out to those who haven't yet experienced that redemption?

And if he is saying those things, then where am I in the process?

When you compare the sheep and the goats, you see that the goats really weren't charged with doing anything wrong. In fact, they just didn't do anything. They were so focused on their own lives, their own comfort and needs and desires, that they ignored the crying needs that surrounded them.

Each crying need has a face. And each of those faces is Christ's face. By ignoring their needs, we are ignoring Christ.

To enter into the eternal realm, we must enter into serving those in need—even those with disgusting, nasty, get-your-hands-dirty kind of needs. When we do, we come face to face with Jesus himself.

Come.

Jesus, help me see your face in every single person I come across today. Use me to help meet somebody's need. Keep me alert to the opportunities you bring before me continually. Amen.

Jesus Beckons You
to Witness

19. What to Do as You Go

As you go, proclaim the good news, "The kingdom of heaven has come near." Cure the sick, raise the dead, cleanse the lepers, cast out demons. You received without payment; give without payment. Take no gold, or silver, or copper in your belts, no bag for your journey, or two tunics, or sandals, or a staff; for laborers deserve their food. Whatever town or village you enter, find out who in it is worthy, and stay there until you leave. As you enter the house, greet it. If the house is worthy, let your peace come upon it; but if it is not worthy, let your peace return to you. —MATTHEW 10:7-13

Jesus makes telling others about him seem so simple.

Meanwhile, in the church today we have all sorts of responses and reactions to the idea of evangelism. Many of us recoil in panic from the very idea. Others create mammoth, highly organized, multimedia campaigns—and somehow the clear, clean, simple message of God's love gets lost in all the hoopla.

Jesus called his twelve disciples to him and gave them a list of very simple imperatives. The first: "Go." There was no doubt associated with his invitation to following him. Just go.

He instructed the disciples to start with their fellow Israelites. I like how Eugene Peterson in *The Message* brought the same command to our modern consciousness: "Go to the lost, confused people right here in the neighborhood."

Know anyone like that, someone who is confused? You are likely surrounded by them. So, go.

You don't have to make a big deal about it. You are going already. You are living your life. You may be out and about every day. So, this is something you do while on your way. As you're going, keep your eyes open for opportunities to approach the lost and confused around you.But how do you do that? What do you do as you go?

✤ Be sensitive to God's Spirit, working in and through you.

✤ Don't be afraid to leave your comfort zone to meet someone who's very different from you and strike up a conversation about life.

✤ Be clear and simple about God's presence with them right now.

✤ Meet any needs you can and be open to receiving their hospitality in turn.

✤ And don't make a big deal about those who don't want to listen to you—just walk away in peace.

It's fairly simple. As you go about your everyday life, be open to any possibility to say a word, to perform an act of kindness, to offer a listening ear, to share the love and presence of God, even a quick prayer.

A friend of mine was able to do this in a unique and powerful way on a trip to South America with his church group. The team wanted to put these verses into practice, to enter a town and seek out those who might be open to their message of God's love. They stayed in modest homes and ate whatever was given to them. And they simply offered to pray with those they met.

"How can I pray for you?" That question always seemed to open the door to a conversation—and for God's Spirit to work.

These encounters revolutionized my friend's life. Though the culture was different, the needs of the people in this other country were the same as those at home—human needs for love and acceptance, for hope and health, needs that dwell at the core of each one of us. He brought his experience back with him in his encounters with people he met throughout his day at work, at his church, and in the neighborhood. My friend got what Jesus was saying. But we do not need to go to South America to experience this, though perhaps we should be open to that. Jesus coaxes us to follow his lead in our own neighborhood, our own spheres of influence.

Why should we do this? Jesus explains: "You received… so give." In other words, God has loved you generously, so live generously. As you go, lavishly share the peace and love of the God who has grabbed hold of your soul. Help bring the kingdom of heaven a little closer to this needy world.

❧

Jesus, you beckon me to go, to reach out and bear witness to your love. What's holding me back? Help me take the first step. Walk with me. Help me to live generously and lavishly—as lavishly as you have been with me. Amen.

20. Shouting from the Housetops

> So have no fear of them; for nothing is covered
> up that will not be uncovered, and nothing
> secret that will not become known. What I
> say to you in the dark, tell in the light; and
> what you hear whispered, proclaim from the
> housetops. —MATTHEW 10:26-27

I'm always amazed and curious when I see a news story about a prominent individual who's caught doing something immoral or illegal.

In the city where I live, an upstanding businessman, active in the community and in his church, was arrested for messing around with his children's underage babysitter. His family, his career, his reputation—his whole life—was turned upside down in a moment.

Once long ago in a church I attended, the truth about the beloved longtime pastor's predatory sexual indiscretions with underage victims finally came to light. The church's board had known about these troubling issues, but they merely slapped his hand and covered it up. When the sordid truth finally emerged, even after the pastor had retired, people felt so shocked, hurt, and betrayed that it led to an emotional split in the church and devastating psychological pain in many members' lives.

Look at some of the major business failures in recent years, and you'll see a persistent trend: leaders not only engaging in illegal activities but doing their best to cover them up. Yet somehow, someone cracks under the pressure of maintaining a falsehood and trying to hide the truth, and the story becomes headline news for months.

We all have things in our lives that would embarrass us if they were reported by the local TV news team. But Jesus is letting us know that, in truth, there really are no secrets. God knows all. We might as well accept the inevitable, confess our failures, and live in light of the consequences.

This truth also has a positive flip side. We are holding on to the most important news humanity has ever known—a secret that so many folks still don't know. It's the secret of God's love, the challenge of following in the way of Jesus, and the knowledge that all will be well eternally in the realm of God.

Why do we keep this wonderful news a secret?

Well, for one thing, when Jesus said this to his disciples, they faced persecution, even death. There was a measure of discretion involved in lying low, in keeping quiet, of speaking in whispers. Many of our brothers and sisters around the world face similar persecution now. They carefully follow their faithful practices, acknowledging the threat but trying not to be stifled by it.

What about you? What would people think of you if they knew you believed in God and wanted to live the way Jesus has been inviting you to live? You might get a cold shoulder or a biting epithet, but I doubt you face physical harm for your faith. So why keep Jesus a secret? "Have no fear," he beckons to you. Don't be intimidated, go public—shout it from the rooftops. Proclaim it wherever you go. It's all going to come out in the end, and everyone will ultimately know the whole truth. You might as well get started sharing the good news now.

∽⊗∾

Jesus, I acknowledge that, compared to many believers around the world, now and in the past, I have it relatively easy. I don't want to keep you a secret. I want to share you, to proclaim you, to shout your love from the rooftops. Help me please. Amen.

21. Coming and Going

Go therefore and make disciples of all
nations, baptizing them in the name of the
Father and of the Son and of the Holy Spirit.
—MATTHEW 28:19

Jesus tells us to go. He seems to say that a lot.

I realize how much better I like his invitations to "come." To come be with him, spend time in his presence, relax in his love and acceptance, soak in his mercy.

But then he tells us, his followers, to go.

Mark's parallel passage puts it this way: "Go into all the world and proclaim the good news to the whole creation" (Mark 16:15).

Don't just go to your neighbors and coworkers. Go into the whole world. Go everywhere. Go far and near. Go sharing the good news with everyone you encounter. Go marking them by the water of baptism. Go with the goal of informing and training and revealing and sharing the way of love.

This way of life possesses a rhythm. It's the rhythm:

- ✤ Of coming and going

- ✤ Of being with Jesus and then taking Jesus to others

- ✤ Of getting filled and then sharing that filling

- ✤ Of drinking in and pouring out

- ✤ Of sabbath rest and work in the world

- ✤ Of learning how to be a disciple and then helping others to be disciples too

All of us move about in our spheres of influence bringing a message. We go out into our communities, our workplaces, our neighborhoods, our family gatherings, and we represent something to others. It may be a message of indifference and self-protection, or it may be a message of the reality of the God-transformed life.

Maybe we don't need to make this a daunting task, which prevents us from doing much of anything. Maybe we don't always have to figure out a discipleship curriculum and an evangelism strategy to fulfill this imperative of Christ's. Maybe, instead, we just need to go out and be open, alert, and available to those opportunities God gives us to say something simple and positive and thought-provoking, to do a simple act of caring and kindness.

But nothing can happen if we don't *go*.

❧

Jesus, you keep calling me. I keep ignoring you, or postponing you, or explaining your call away. Today, I want to go for you. I need your help. Amen.

22. What to Do After You Go

> [Teach] them to obey everything that I
> have commanded you. And remember, I
> am with you always, to the end of the age.
> —MATTHEW 28:20

Jesus has told us to *go* into the world (Matthew 28:19), wherever we are, and introduce him to everyone we meet. But what do we do *after* we go?

I used to have a skewed, awkward, and even rude understanding of this. In college, I was involved with a conservative evangelical campus ministry that encouraged us to share a few little steps to enable those we approached to become Christian. If they didn't accept Jesus, we would, after a bit of a guilt-tripping, walk away. Leave them, ignore them as lost causes. If they decided to follow Christ, then we'd just train them to do the same thing we were without any real understanding of who Jesus was or what he calls us to be and do.

Rather than that approach, Jesus has another imperative for us, another command, another invitation: "Teach them to obey everything that I have commanded you."

Don't just leave the folks you meet high and dry. Form relationships. Become friends. Show them how to live by following Jesus. Teach them the way of Christ. Introduce them to the beauties and riches of relationship with God.

This isn't a one-time event. It's a way of life. It's day after day after day. Jesus calls us to get into the world and get busy getting the word out, transfering our knowledge, our understanding, and our relationship with God to others.

That means being with people. Spending time with them. Listening to them. Learning from them. And encouraging them to do to the same thing with others in their own spheres of influence.

It sounds like a huge job, a mammoth responsibility. It is.

It is what Christianity is all about.

And—don't forget, Jesus says—it comes with a promise: "I am with you always, to the end of the age."

These are the final words of Jesus that Matthew records in his gospel story. They are good words to let echo in our minds and hearts, and to take with us every step of every day. Jesus is always with us. Wherever we are. Right with us in our hearts and lives, our pains and problems, our loneliness and laziness, our fears and frustrations. He is there.

And he'll never leave us. He'll never forget us. He'll never ignore us. He'll work to help us grow up in the faith, grow stronger in his love. And he will be here with you doing this every day. Until the very end.

❧

Jesus, does my life look like this picture you've painted of a faithful follower? One who goes out bringing you to everyone I meet? One who teaches and encourages and challenges? One who trusts that you are with me every step of the way? I want to accept this challenge, this call. By faith I do so. Thank you for being with me as I do. Amen.

Jesus Beckons You to Boldness

23. Come Ahead

> Peter answered him, "Lord, if it is you,
> command me to come to you on the water."
> He said, "Come." So Peter got out of the boat,
> started walking on the water, and came toward
> Jesus. —Matthew 14:28-29a

⬦

While fishing, the disciples caught sight of something bizarre. Their teacher was coming toward them.

Walking.

On the water.

Note how Eugene Peterson captures the scene in *The Message*: "Peter, suddenly bold, said, 'Master, if it's really you, call me to come to you on the water.'"

Notice first that Peter is "suddenly bold." You know that feeling, don't you—an unexpected opportunity pops up, and you just go for it. You don't even have time to think of the ramifications or the possible consequences. You just feel suddenly bold and step out.

Maybe somebody gives you an opportunity to say something personal and profound about God in your life. Maybe somebody calls for an emergency volunteer to visit a person in the hospital and, though you are tired and busy, you say yes. Maybe you see a worker being treated unfairly by an employer, and you speak up for what's just. Maybe you're given an opportunity to take part in an opportunity to serve others and, rather than come up with all the usual excuses, you just trust God and go.

It could be a million things. But they're all unexpected opportunities. And it's the Spirit of God within you that quickens your heart to become "suddenly bold."

And yet, as bold as Peter was, he still had some doubt: "Lord, if it is you…"

He wasn't sure. After all, his companions thought it was a ghost coming toward them on the water. Yes, it looked like Jesus, but—was he really walking on the water? So, Peter put this apparition coming toward him to the test: "Command me to come to you on the water."

Now, isn't that just a little silly? Wanting to walk on the water? Playing games with Jesus about it? Oh yes. But wouldn't it be fun? And, besides, Jesus encouraged us to come to God as little children. If we could, we'd be slipping and sliding and dancing and jumping all over the surface of the water, wouldn't we? Admit it.

Peter gave in to that simple, fun wish. He wanted to go play with Jesus in the water. And Jesus's response was, well, so Jesus. Simple. Clear. Direct. Assuring. Accepting. "Come."

Could Jesus be saying the same thing to you? Is he beckoning you into unknown waters? You've been wanting to step out of the boat of safety and security, the boat of the status quo, and go for it, whatever God is calling you to. You feel that boldness bubbling up at unexpected times, and you so want to climb out of that boat and do something extraordinary, for Jesus.

And yet, there's that doubt: "Is it really you, Lord?"

But Jesus still says, "Come."

Once Jesus answered his question, Peter didn't hesitate. He didn't consider the odds. He didn't calculate the chances. He didn't ponder the laws of physics.

He jumped. And walked right toward his beckoning friend.

Oh, if only the story had ended right there. Wouldn't you feel more ready to jump out too if you knew Peter raced around the fishing boat while his shocked companions witnessed the impossible before their very eyes?

Alas, the next two verses reveal what happened: "But when he looked down at the waves churning beneath his feet, he lost his nerve and started to sink. He cried, 'Master, save me!'"

Jesus didn't hesitate. He reached down and grabbed his hand. Then he said, "Faint-heart, what got into you?" (Matthew 14:30-31, *The Message*).

Peter stopped looking at Jesus, and he started looking down. He lost his nerve, his faith, his boldness. He started to sink. You probably know that feeling. I know I do. You clearly hear God calling you, but then so-called "reality" sets in and slaps you sideways.

Wait a minute, you think. This can't be right. I can't be doing this! I'm not strong enough or wise enough or gifted enough or called enough to be doing this. Who do I think I am, anyway?

Jesus's loving response to Peter gives us insight into the way he will respond to us. He didn't let Peter drown. Instead, he grabbed him and pulled him up. You can almost hear Jesus chuckle as he gently chided his hapless disciple.

In those times when you doubt, when you are sinking beneath the waves, Jesus says the same to you: "Faint-heart, what got into you?"

I say, let's not get bogged down in the wet finale of this wonderful story. Let's focus on that initial boldness, that fresh desire to do something beyond our safety zone with and for our Savior, who beckons us to "come." If you take that first step out of your boat toward your inviting Savior, keeping your eyes locked on him and his calling for you, what might happen? If you get a little wet, so what? Jesus is there. Pulling you up.

Jesus, you beckon me onto the waters of abundant living, coaxing me to risk stepping out of my familiar security—boldly. You stand there waiting for me. Can I come to you? Can I trust you? Do I dare take that step of faith? Amen.

24. Prayerful Persistence

> So I say to you, Ask, and it will be given you; search, and you will find; knock, and the door will be opened for you. For everyone who asks receives, and everyone who searches finds, and for everyone who knocks, the door will be opened. —LUKE 11:9-10

⁂

Kids tend to be very good at following Jesus's invitation here. Jesus encourages us to come to God as little children, so maybe we can learn something from them.

When they were young, my two kids were hardly unusual in their application of the persistence principle. If they wanted something, they would ask, cajole, argue, rationalize, and keep on asking until I either gave in or blew up. Maybe they wanted to go to the park, or see a movie, or go swimming. If I said "No" firmly, they usually got the message. But if I said, "We'll see" or "Maybe later," they were relentless.

Jesus tells us that when we pray, we need to be relentless, to keep asking, seeking, and knocking. Persistence is an important part of prayer. This isn't about trying to play games with God, trying to trick, convince, or bargain with God, or wear God down with our obstinacy. Jesus simply invites us to be direct. Ask for what we want. And keep asking for it if need be.

One of the things I've learned over the years is to ask for what I want. I am, by nature, a prime example of one who beats around the bush, hinting, hoping someone will figure out what I need without my having to actually ask for it— and passive-aggressively punishing someone for not reading my mind.

I remember as a boy riding in the back seat of our family car while Dad drove us all home after church or some other family outing. Rather than ask Dad directly and thereby possibly receive a brusque no, I would attempt to send him mental commands via ESP: *"Let's stop by Nick's News so I can buy the latest comic books... let's go to Nick's News... we must stop by Nick's News... Nick's News...."*

It didn't work very often, I can assure you. Unlike my father, God knows our minds yet still tells us to ask for what we need or want.

Over the years, I have been amazed by what happens when I ask for what I need boldly, directly, and clearly, without dancing around or pretending I'm asking for something else.

That's Jesus's point. God's answer may be "no." Or it may be "We'll see." But unless we are bold enough to ask, we'll never get to "yes."

⬥

Jesus, you model for us an honesty and boldness that I would love to see in my own life. I want this. And I'm asking for it. And I will keep asking for it, seeking it, knocking at the door of heaven for it, because this is the way you've called me to live. Thank you for the challenge. Amen.

25. Stand Up

> Now when these things begin to take place,
> stand up and raise your heads, because your
> redemption is drawing near. —LUKE 21:28

❧

Wars. Nations fighting nations. Earthquakes. Famines. Pandemics.

Vicious persecution. Lawsuits. Police harassment. Family betrayal.

All hell breaking loose.

Then… then…!

Then they will see "the Son of Man coming in cloud with power and great glory" (Luke 21:27).

Jesus tells his followers and friends that this is what they have to look forward to. Some of it already seems to be unfolding day by day as the clouds seem to grow darker in our world. It isn't a pretty picture. In fact, it's downright terrifying.

If, as a believer you faced the prospect of all sorts of persecution, harassment, betrayal, even imprisonment, even death, how would you feel? Would you want to run away and hide? Would you want to protect yourself? Avoid bringing attention to yourself? Slink away, out of sight, your eyes downcast in fear and humiliation?

Jesus has a word for you: "Stand up and raise your heads."

Don't look down. Don't hide. Don't run away. Be bold. Stand tall. Look up. And see the help that's on the way.

We can get bogged down in the various theories regarding the "Day of Vengeance" or the end times. We get so bogged down we can't hear Jesus's generous beckoning to us.

It's a word of bold hope when life seems meaningless.

It's a word of bold faith when the world seems out of control.

It's a word of bold trust when circumstances seem formidable.

It's a word of bold love when your situation feels cold and empty.

It may not be the end of the world, but it sure may feel like it to you. Don't slink away. Don't look down. Don't hide. Don't give up.

Jesus is coming. Help is on the way. Just look up and see.

Jesus, the world seems to be going to hell. And my corner of the world—my own life—often seems just as frightening as the world situation. Thank you for promising to be there for me, to bring all the help I need. Give me the strength, even when surrounded by pain and fear, disappointment and destruction, to stand up with my head held high. Trusting you. Seeing you. Knowing you are with me. Amen.

26. A Fearless Endurance

> Do not fear what you are about to suffer.
> Beware, the devil is about to throw some of
> you into prison so that you may be tested, and
> for ten days you will have affliction. Be faithful
> until death, and I will give you the crown of
> life. —REVELATION 2:10

A car parked near mine at my condo garage sports a "No Fear" sticker on the rear window. I walk by that car at least once a day. Whenever I see that sticker, I have to wonder whether the owner of the car is really sane. No fear? In this life? On this planet? Are you crazy?

You must be emotionally dead not to possess some sense of fear in what might happen, not only to you personally but also in the world. The next second could bring a catastrophe of immense proportions. Or not. And the waiting and wondering whether that catastrophe is about to hit can make us crazy.

What if someone very close to you is hit by a car? What if that bonus check you were counting on balancing your accounts doesn't materialize? What if you're stricken by illness and unable to fulfill your responsibilities?

Oh, we can come up with an infinite number of things to be fearful of.

So, when someone boldly claims in a bumper sticker that they ain't afraid of nothing, I am a bit suspect. I think they must simply be putting on a way-cool, tough-guy act, and deep down inside they're afraid of something.

Then I read this passage, in which Jesus gently beckons me simply, "Do not fear."

It seems too good to be true. Just don't fear? Is Jesus promising that I never have to fear anything? That I am so blessed and protected, there's no need to be fearful? Just "do not fear," and he will handle everything?

No. That's not the full message.

"Do not fear what you are about to suffer."

The suffering *is* coming. The testing *is* coming. It may even cost us our life—so Jesus tells the church. But you don't have to fear it.

He also invites us to "Be faithful unto death." Keep the faith. Don't lose hope. Stay strong in the knowledge that you are God's child, God's beloved forever.

In these words from Revelation, Jesus tells the church at Smyrna that the suffering they are about to experience won't last forever, but their relationship with Christ will. And they will be well cared for, even lauded with a crown of life, for their suffering on his behalf.

This makes me feel very small. I have no concept, personally, of the suffering these siblings of ours must have endured. Yet I am fearful about the stupidest, smallest, most insignificant things.

Why can't I accept Christ's invitation to trust him boldly? Why can't I set my fears aside and enter into whatever awaits me, knowing that it will all work out in the end?

⌘

Jesus, my trust is weak, my fear is strong. Your Spirit can reverse that, if I open myself to you. Help me to enter into your will, as fully and as boldly as I possibly can, trusting you. Amen.

Jesus Beckons You to Readiness

27. Stay Woke

> Keep awake therefore, for you do not
> know on what day your Lord is coming.
> —MATTHEW 24:42

It seems we have little trouble keeping awake in these times.

The nonstop "breaking news" on cable and the "Alert!" headlines filling our social media timelines keep us up-to-date with every painful nuance of human existence in the world today. In a moment's time, we can access the latest reports from the world's hot spots on our cell phones and watch split-screen discussions and angry debates on whatever happens to be the breathless news story of the moment.

Yes, we do keep awake to what's going on around us.

On the other hand, being truly awake to reality in these tense times seems more difficult than ever. Our senses are exhausted from all this anxious alertness. We are numb after years of fear and concern and uncertainty. Our feelings have shut down from fatigue. We just want to get away from it all. Turn it off.

In a time of utter awakeness, we are in many ways less woke than ever. Less alert to the ultimate realities—the realities of our heart. Our personal relationships. Our dependence on God for every moment of every day.

We slip into a deadness of soul. We've worked so hard to protect ourselves from pain and suffering, from experiencing the sheer razor-edged terror of life in a world that's separated from God, that we have trouble really feeling, being awake to what's true and right and real.

While our eyes are wide open, we cover them lest we see the truth of our needy, decaying souls. While our ears react to every alarm sounded by the media, we shut them up lest we hear the still, small voice of God beckoning to us, calling us to stay awake, to be alert.

In her book *The Last American Man*, Elizabeth Gilbert tells the true story of Eustace Conway, who left his dysfunctional suburban family at age seventeen to live off the land in the wilds of Appalachia. Ultimately, he amassed a thousand acres of property near Boone, North Carolina, and taught children and adults the ways of nature.

One young man named Dave, desperate for attention after his parents divorced, came to spend some time at the Turtle Island compound to learn how to live in the wild and become a man:

> Eustace used his time with Dave to try to have him understand the fundamental essence of his philosophy, which centered on mindfulness. There is no way, Eustace said to Dave, that you can have a decent life as a man if you aren't awake and aware every moment. Show up for your own life, he said. Don't pass your days in a stupor, content to swallow whatever watery ideas modern society may bottle-feed you through the media, satisfied to slumber through life in an instant-gratification sugar coma. The most extraordinary gift you've been given is your own humanity, which is about consciousness, so honor that consciousness....
>
> Be awake, Eustace said (laughing at the very simplicity of it), and you will succeed in this world. When it rains, find shelter! When you're being stung by yellow jackets, run! Only through constant focus can you become independent. Only through independence can you know yourself. And only through knowing yourself will you be able to ask the key questions of your life: *What is it that I am destined to accomplish, and how can I make it happen?*

That's a good reminder to pay attention, to stay woke. But why does Jesus coax us to stay awake and alert? So we can be ready. Ready for him. Ready for what's really important: the presence of Jesus in our midst.

Jesus has promised to return. How, when, and where are the subjects of theological debates that echo through the centuries since Jesus was here the first time in the flesh. Nevertheless, the time is coming.

Jesus tells us to Watch. Listen. Stay awake. Be alert. Wait for his presence with us in the world.

When we do that, we won't be distracted by all the negativity the world has to throw at us. And we'll be ready for whatever way Jesus shows up in front of us—whatever face he wears— ready to love and to serve.

We have no idea how or when we will meet Jesus face to face. Jesus invites us to start getting ready now. Stay woke.

⚭

Jesus, sometimes I feel deadened and detached from reality. It's so easy to slip into unconsciousness. Please, wake me up. I want to be ready for you, whenever and however you show up in my life. Amen.

28. *Ready for Anything*

> Be dressed for action and have your lamps lit;
> be like those who are waiting for their master to
> return from the wedding banquet, so that they
> may open the door for him as soon as he comes
> and knocks. —LUKE 12:35-36

❧

I like to be punctual. It upsets me to be late. And it frustrates me no end to not be ready for an event when it's scheduled to begin.

When I travel, knowing I have an early flight or a sunrise breakfast meeting, I will often set two alarms just in case to allow me plenty of time to get up and get ready.

I'm not alone. A friend of mine is similarly lateness-resistant, and he was telling me this penchant has brought a certain amount of relational zest to his marriage, as his wife tends to be, shall we say, time-challenged. In fact, he often urges his wife to explore and overcome her apparent fear of being on time. But after more than 25 years of marriage, he is finally getting used to being late at times.

At any rate, when I read Jesus's invitation in Luke's Gospel, it resonates with me. I want to be ready for him. I do not want to oversleep and miss the blessing.

Jesus promises he will surprise us. He will show up when we least expect it, when we're distracted by the mundane activities of our lives. He encourages us to wait up for him, no matter how late it is—dressed and alert and listening intently for that knock on the door.

Despite my desire to be punctual, I also love my sleep. I am an early-to-bed-and-early-to-rise kind of person. And if I don't get my necessary seven or eight hours of sleep, beware.

So, am I supposed to stay up all night for the Lord? Let's not be so literal. This isn't about being on time or staying up all night waiting. It's about being ready, eager, prepared to respond to God's entrance into our lives at a moment's notice. That means making sure we're living as God has called us to live. Fulfilling our God-given responsibilities as followers of Jesus. Exercising our gifts and pursuing our calling. Being ready for anything.

When you open the door and see an opportunity staring you in the face—like the servants' master in these verses from Luke—will you be ready? Maybe the door opens to an opportunity to help someone in need, or mentor a neglected child, or teach an English as a Second Language class, or share a word of comfort with a grieving heart, or encourage a truth-seeker to find meaning in a relationship with God—some unexpected, surprising, God-given opportunity to follow Jesus in the way of love.

Are you prepared to be flexible enough to change your schedule or adjust your mindset or open your heart to it? Jesus says: "If he comes during the middle of the night, or near dawn, and finds them [ready], blessed are those [servants]" (Luke 12:38).

Be awake. Be ready. And be blessed.

Jesus, build in me an attitude of readiness, of openness to your unexpected visits with me through other people. I want to be responsive to the God-appointments in my life and not so tied up in all the details of my own schedule that I miss the eternal blessings you want to surprise me with. Amen.

29. Awakened Ears

Let anyone who has an ear listen to what
the Spirit is saying to the churches.
—REVELATION 2:7

❧

We are surrounded by noise.

If I step outside my condo in Midtown Atlanta, the noise
can be nearly deafening at times. There is all sorts of traffic,
engines racing, horns blaring, tires squealing. I live directly
across from a fire station—which is great if our condo ever
catches on fire but brings with it lots of siren and horn noise.
And underneath it all is a constant roar, the endless cacophony
of the city awake.

Even at a cabin in remote Western North Carolina, the noises
can be constant: lawn mowers, trucks climbing the mountain
highway, construction activity up the street complete with
buzz saws and hammers, various neighbors' dogs apparently
arguing over some fine point of canine philosophy.

And in my own head, the noises rarely abate. They are the
myriad of thoughts and worries and reminders and questions.
And do you ever have a song get stuck in your head and replay

over and over again? That's been happening to me today—thankfully the current number on my cranial jukebox is a good old hymn. Most of the time it's an annoying ditty I picked up on TV or the radio. I want to unplug that inner jukebox, but sometimes it seems impossible.

I read Jesus's words to the church at Ephesus, and I want so much to tune out all the other noises so I can listen. I want to wake up my spiritual ears, so the Spirit can whisper into my heart.

Like me, you've probably experienced great frustration because God isn't speaking to you. You want to hear God, but there's nothing there. Just a vast silence.

Or so it seems. Maybe the Spirit is there all along, whispering, wooing, coaxing—but our ears are not awake to it. We're so focused instead on all the other noises of life—both external and internal—that we simply cannot hear.

How do we wake up our ears? How do we listen?

Sometimes, I think we try too hard. We sit on the edge of our seats and strain to hear that still, small voice. Maybe we should simply relax. We could accept the fact that there are a lot of noises in our lives that we must make peace with, even welcome into our awareness, and ask God to awaken our ears so we can recognize that the Spirit is speaking, if we would only pay attention.

I was sitting on my patio thinking and praying about what to write today, noticing all the noises around me in my urban neighborhood. It took several minutes before I realized a peaceful sound underneath all the other sounds of everyday life—a sound that was nearly drowned out and so indistinct that I had to consciously realize it was there. It was the sound of the breeze through the leaves of the trees around me. A very slight breeze, but nearly constant. The sound of the wind.

I had to wake up my ears to hear the gentle, clean rustle of the green—just as I have to wake up my ears to hear the whispered words of God's Spirit. Listen. Can you hear them too? Are you ready to act on them?

❧

Jesus, you invite me to listen to the living Spirit of God within me and around me. But I confess that so often, my ears are closed or filled with the meaningless cacophony of the mundane. Open my ears. I want to hear your whispered words of love and wisdom and calling and strength. Speak to me and let the Spirit blow through me. Amen.

Jesus Beckons You into His Presence

30. Pray Like This

> Your Father knows what you need before you
> ask him. Pray then in this way: Our Father in
> heaven, hallowed be your name. Your kingdom
> come. Your will be done, on earth as it is in
> heaven. Give us this day our daily bread. And
> forgive us our debts, as we also have forgiven
> our debtors. And do not bring us to the time of
> trial, but rescue us from the evil one.
> —Matthew 6:8-13

We know this prayer so well, don't we? Or do we?

Jesus invites you to pray with him like this: Simply. Knowing that God your holy parent knows you better than you know yourself, knows exactly what's best for you.

When you trust this God, prayer is simple.

You acknowledge the real presence of God.

You ask God to reveal who God is.

You ask God to set the world right, doing what's best in heaven and on earth.

You ask for your physical necessities and trust God to provide what you need as God does for the birds and the flowers.

You ask for God's forgiveness and the ability to forgive others who have hurt you.

You ask for safety and security from your own weaknesses and failures, as well as from the temptations of evil.

And you acknowledge God's authority, power, and glory forever.

Simple. It covers all the bases with clarity and directness.

So why do we try so hard to complicate the matter? Why is it so often a drudgery to pray? Why do we feel we need to attend seminars and read weighty tomes on prayer? It's not that those things will hurt us or hinder our ability to pray. But sometimes we feel we need to figure it all out before we even try.

Of course, there are those times in life when you simply don't feel like praying. You can't seem to put two prayerful words together in any way that makes sense.

Many years ago, following particularly rough times regarding my job, my church, my friends, and even my family all at once, a time when I even questioned the existence of God, I found the concept of prayer to be impossible. I simply couldn't even read the Bible. It all seemed meaningless and empty. How could I pray to a God who had allowed all this chaos into my life?

Slowly, tentatively, after long weeks passed, I began to be able to talk to God about all this. Simply, directly, just as Jesus has invited us here. Often, I would pray out loud, while driving or in a quiet place alone. That helped immensely.

Now I look back on that time as essential in my own spiritual growth. It was a time when I could shake out all the heartless assumptions that I had based my faith on, assumptions that turned out not to be very authentic in my own life. A time when I could begin to build a relationship with God that was as honest and true as I could be. A time to question and doubt and rebuild on a strong, sturdy foundation of trustworthy faith. A time to realistically understand that I will never, ever have everything all figured out.

If I had not gone through all that, I would still be living a shallow, false, superficial religion that had no relationship with the reality within my soul. I wouldn't have ended up where I am today—with such a long, long way still to go yet with an experience of God as real as my relationship with my spouse or a friend or a grandchild.

Do you feel like praying today? Do you feel like coming close to God?

Take a moment to pray through Eugene Peterson's astonishing translation of this text:

> This is your Father you are dealing with, and he knows better than you what you need. With a God like this loving you, you can pray very simply. Like this:

> "Our Father in heaven,
> Reveal who you are.
> Set the world right;
> Do what's best—as above, so below.
> Keep us alive with three square meals.
> Keep us forgiven with you and forgiving others.
> Keep us safe from ourselves and the Devil.
> You're in charge!
> You can do anything you want!
> You're ablaze in beauty!
>   Yes. Yes. Yes."

> (Matthew 6:8b-13, *The Message*)

No matter how far away you may feel from God, you can draw close with this simple prayer, knowing that you are praying to a God who knows you completely and still loves you totally.

A God who hears you and knows what's best for you, now and in the long run.

A God who yearns deeply for your company in open, honest, loving conversation.

A God who can't wait to answer your prayers and work in abounding ways in your life.

Yes. Yes. Yes.

ॐ

God, I thank you that you know me thoroughly and accept me completely. I thank you for the privilege of prayer. I want to spend time with you now, talking things over, acknowledging your presence and provision. Amen.

31. A Peaceful Burden

> Come to me, all you that are weary and are
> carrying heavy burdens, and I will give you rest.
> Take my yoke upon you, and learn from me;
> for I am gentle and humble in heart, and you
> will find rest for your souls. For my yoke is easy,
> and my burden is light. —MATTHEW 11:28-30

These are some of the most beautiful words of invitation ever heard.

How I yearn to come closer and relax in Jesus's presence. How thirsty I am for his company, to be alone with him.

I haven't always felt this way. Going away somewhere by myself just didn't seem to fit my personality. I love my spouse, love being with him and going places with him. I enjoy the company of friends and family. Why would I go somewhere by myself? Would I drive myself crazy? Would I be bored to tears, unable to do anything constructive, incapable of opening up to God?

I decided to find out during Lent some years ago. I truly wanted to meet with God to get a fresh sense of direction for my life. So, I arranged to stay in a cabin next to a rocky, rolling creek at Camp Mikell, the Episcopal conference center in North Georgia.

On the covered porch overlooking the rambunctious creek, sitting in a rocking chair in front of Room 701 in Mikell Village, I cataloged my feelings. I felt chilly—it was March 12, so the weather was still cool.

I also felt frazzled after a long, hard, nonstop day at work. My plans to leave the office early and take a leisurely drive two hours north of Atlanta were dashed when a last-minute emergency project hit at work. Even so, I left the office late while others labored into the night, so I was feeling guilty, too.

I was also scared, unsettled. Even though I had made the trip to the campgrounds several times before, I had gotten lost on the way up in the dark. But now I was starting to feel safe. And a little hopeful. Even though I had no idea what I would do or what would happen, I was just going to play it by ear.

When I wrote my journal entry, I had just read Evening Prayer in the Book of Common Prayer and found it moving and refreshing. Maybe this would work after all.

Saturday morning, after a restful night's sleep, I started with Morning Prayer, another beloved moment of praying the hours in the liturgical tradition. In the confession, the phrase "and what we have left undone" struck me. I was feeling as though

my life was full of "left undones." A series of verses came to me
as I read the prayer book.

> "For he is our God, and we are the people of his
> pasture, and the sheep of his hand. Oh, that today you
> would hearken to his voice!" (Psalm 95:7)

> "So teach us to number our days that we may apply
> our hearts to wisdom." (Psalm 90:12)

> "May the graciousness of the LORD our God be
> upon us; prosper the work of our hands; prosper our
> handiwork!" (Psalm 90:17)

> "Whoever is from God hears the words of God. The
> reason you do not hear them is that you are not from
> God." (John 8:47)

As verse tumbled upon verse, I found myself weeping. I
remember almost viscerally sensing the embrace of Jesus. My
simple notes, hardly able to capture the depth of renewal I felt,
read: "Overcome by the love and presence of Jesus! Weeping
tears of love and joy—not sadness. Feel accepted and loved
and cherished like a friend and lover."

Finally, another verse came to me:

> "God can do anything, you know—far more than you
> could ever imagine or guess or request in your wildest
> dreams! He does it not by pushing us around but by

working within us, his Spirit deeply and gently within us.

> Glory to God in the church!
> Glory to God in the Messiah, in Jesus!
> Glory down all the generations!
> Glory through all millennia! Oh, yes!"
> (Ephesians 3:20-21, *The Message*)

This experience carried on through the rest of my retreat weekend and helped me begin the hard process of opening my heart and my eyes to God's wider will for my life—and a painful but ultimately life-giving journey to where I am today.

Two years later during another Lent, I went on another personal retreat, staying in a peaceful yellow cottage a short walk from the Atlantic shoreline on the East Beach of St. Simons Island, Georgia. I was a week away from starting my new job at the *Protestant Hour* (now *Day 1*)—with an overwhelming increase of responsibility—and I wanted to become re-centered with God to prepare myself for it.

I wrote on March 8 of that year in my journal:

Here I am. Thursday morning in the cottage. Gorgeous morning—but cold.

Here I am. A week from today I will be executive producer of *The Protestant Hour*. The change will be traumatic, but I'm so excited. So much to do. Overwhelming.

Here I am. Kind of empty. Scared. Surfacey. I have kept busy here, maybe too busy....

Here I am: *Me*. Oh God, how I need you. Who do I think I am? Have I defrauded these people? Thank you, God, for bringing me to this place.

Part of that retreat, and three more annual Lenten retreats after that one to the same lovely little cottage, involved another discipline: painting a Station of the Cross for my parish's annual display. Every year, the many talented artists who belong to the church select a particular station to paint.

I found this exercise not only physically and mentally challenging but also emotionally moving and faith building. As I paint on a large canvas the image of Christ carrying the cross or being stripped of his clothes or dying on the cross, I can't help but feel pulled into the act, becoming part of it, sensing how it felt, wondering how I would have responded and desiring Jesus's presence.

Retreats such as these are times when I can take up Jesus's invitation in Matthew 11:28-30, times when I can get away from the dry routine, exhaustion, and even burnout of life and come to Jesus. During these times, I am able to get away with Jesus and recover my life, to experience real rest in his presence, walking with him, working with him, seeing how he does things, and trying to follow along.

I desperately want to learn from Jesus and find rest for my soul. And with my time stripped of responsibility and distraction and interference, I have a better opportunity to do that. While these times of retreat can be powerful and life changing, I can trust that Jesus won't put any burden too heavy on me, anything that doesn't fit my personality and gifts.

Jesus beckons generously to each of us: "Come to me… and rest."

∞

Jesus, I want to keep company with you. I want to learn to live freely and lightly. I want to be able to sense your embrace not only on those too infrequent retreats, but here. Now. Today. Right in the midst of this routine life you have led me into. Amen.

32. Take

> While they were eating, he took a loaf of bread,
> and after blessing it he broke it, gave it to them,
> and said, "Take; this is my body." —MARK 14:22

⌘

Jesus and his closest friends, his most devoted, very human followers, gather for a final meal together. Perhaps they will celebrate Passover and remember the deliverance of the nation of Israel from Egypt, when the angel of death passed over them, giving them the opportunity to leave the land of their bondage.

With just a few simple words, Jesus transforms their perceptions.

The Book of Common Prayer (Eucharistic Rite II) summarizes the scene this way:

> On the night he was handed over to suffering and death, our Lord Jesus Christ took bread; and when he had given thanks to you, he broke it, and gave it to his disciples, and said, "Take, eat: This is my Body, which is given for you. Do this for the remembrance of me."

As Jesus hands them the unleavened bread, he tells them it is his body. Take it. Eat it. "Get hold of it," *Strong's Concordance* offers as one definition of the imperative verb here. In other words, make it yours. Make it *you.*

When Jesus gives them the cup of wine, he says it is his blood. Again, in the Book of Common Prayer:

> After supper he took the cup of wine; and when
> he had given thanks, he gave it to them, and said,
> "Drink this, all of you: This is my Blood of the new
> Covenant, which is shed for you and for many for the
> forgiveness of sins. Whenever you drink it, do this for
> the remembrance of me."

The disciples all drink from it. They taste the sweetness and the bitterness; they inhale the wine's musky aroma, the pungent bouquet. They experience the warmth of it entering their inmost being.

His body, his blood: With you whenever you eat these simple staples of daily nourishment.

His body, his blood: In your presence whenever you gather in fellowship around the table.

His body, his blood: Alive. Within you. Nourishing you. Present with you always.

Not just bread and wine. Not just body and blood. But Jesus. Alive. Present. Now.

Jesus warns his gathered friends in that upper room that the darkest day in earth's history is coming, tomorrow. But he will be with them, day in and day out, forever. All they must do is remember.

"Do this for the remembrance of me."

Every time they eat bread and drink wine, they will be reminded of this truth. Reminded of their beloved Lord's presence. Within them. And so it can be with you.

Think back about all the communion services you've been part of. Several drift through my mind: A college Sunday school class. A noontime service in a downtown church attracting a dozen or so folks who work in nearby office towers. The final gathering of a church retreat at a rustic conference center. A service for residents of a nursing home. Regular Sunday morning eucharists in a parish where I worship and serve. At a large national denominational convention, serving thousands. In my seminary chapel with fellow students. In a men's Friday morning Bible study. At my wedding with my beloved spouse.

On and on the memories come, going back to my childhood, coming forward to last Sunday. Each one, time after time, is a reminder. Remember Jesus. Remember his presence within you. Remember his fellowship around the table with you. Remember his self-sacrificing love within and among you.

Take. Eat, drink. And remember.

❧

Jesus, I want to grab hold of you and never let you go. And yet, you promise always to be with me. Remind me of your constant presence, your sacrificial love, your eternal provision. Amen.

33. *Holding On*

Hold fast to what you have until I come.
—REVELATION 2:25

Jesus sends a letter from heaven to the church at Thyatira because many of the believers there have gotten way off track and are involved in all sorts of wrong-headed approaches to God under the guidance of a false teacher he calls Jezebel.

Jesus beckons to the remaining faithful in Thyatira who are surrounded by a culture of wanton depravity and utter selfishness, a society whose primary pursuit is self-satisfaction and self-promotion. They are out to get whatever they could, no matter how it hurt themselves or others. And God's Word has gotten lost in the shuffle.

Sounds a little familiar, doesn't it?

Jesus encourages those caught in the maelstrom of faithlessness to hold on. Hold fast to what you have by faith. Grab hold of God's way. Embrace it. And hold tight. You have everything you need to know for this life. God has given you truth that can set you free, direction that can give you purpose, encouragement that can help you survive. It's all in God's

Word. And it's communicated to you through the Spirit. Hold on to God's truth. Get to know it better. Trust it. Rest in it.

Because Jesus is coming for you. And when he gets here, everything that's wrong will be made right. Everything that's upside down will be turned right side up. Everything that's backward will be turned forward. Everything that's empty will be filled to overflowing.

Knowing this, hold fast. Jesus invites you, challenges you, to hold fast to what you know is true. Hold fast to Jesus.

⟡

Jesus, the world is suffocating me with its emptiness, its misdirection, its falseness. It seems to try so hard to force me to turn away, to let go of what I know is right. No matter what I encounter in this struggle-filled world, hold me in your strong arms and give me the strength to grab on to you. And hold on forever. Amen.

III

THE
INDWELLING SPIRIT
AND YOU

*God the Spirit's Invitations to You
from the Epistles*

The Spirit Beckons You to Wholehearted Living

1. Don't Hold Back

> Therefore, do not let sin exercise dominion in your mortal bodies, to make you obey their passions. No longer present your members to sin as instruments of wickedness, but present yourselves to God as those who have been brought from death to life, and present your members to God as instruments of righteousness. —ROMANS 6:12-13

Being an authentic follower of Christ in the power of the Holy Spirit requires a total change of thinking, a turning around from back to front.

On the one hand, the Spirit invites us to let go of every last vestige, habit, or hint of the old way of living. We have to stop hanging around places or people or things that pull our focus away from the way of love. We are so used to living self-centered, self-gratifying lives that this can be a huge and daunting task. We couldn't possibly do it in our own power. That's where the Spirit comes in.

The problem is, often we become so obsessed with living sin-free lives, swatting down every outbreak of an unholy thought with a holy smack, that we never have time to pursue the other side of the equation that Paul gives us here. We never get around to presenting ourselves to God—throwing ourselves wholeheartedly into God's way of doing things.

I have a feeling that if we would focus on that part—the positive invitation to give ourselves over to resurrected living, to the vibrant pursuit of God—the unholy parts of life would take care of themselves.

I had a friend in college who was active in the same conservative Christian organization I participated in. It was a growing, supportive community of students that met in small groups through the week. My friend was a relatively new believer and, frankly, got a little bogged down in Bible verses such as Romans 6:12. As a result, he spent inordinate amounts of time in his dorm room reading the Bible and agonizing over past faults, ways he'd hurt people, and a few colorful sins he'd committed in his youth—which hadn't been that long ago at the time.

With a goal to making amends, forgiving oneself, and moving on, this is a righteous thing to do. But after a few weeks of this, several of us became concerned about our friend. Anytime we would invite him to catch a movie or go to a basketball game or even meet for prayer, he would turn us down. It seemed his sinful predilections were depressing him. He would pray and pray for release from the "old way of life," but he never felt free. In fear of failure, he rarely even ventured from his room.

Thank God, something finally broke through his thinking, and he relaxed and embraced the fact that as a human he would indeed make mistakes from time to time. Somehow, he realized that, as Paul reminds us here, we've been raised from the dead. He could take steps to avoid doing harm to himself or others, but God accepted him in Christ as righteous nevertheless—and wanted to love him just as he was.

Present yourself to God—throw yourself fully and unreservedly into God's arms, into God's way of life. And don't let anything, even your mistakes, hold you back.

❧

Holy Spirit, guide me into a more mature understanding of righteousness and my need for it. Help me to accept my humanity but rely on your power. I want to leap into your will for me, wholeheartedly pursuing your radical way of life, without looking back. Amen.

2. Testing Yourself

> Examine yourselves to see whether you are
> living in the faith. Test yourselves. Do you
> not realize that Jesus Christ is in you? —unless,
> indeed, you fail to pass the test!
> —2 CORINTHIANS 13:5

⬧

How real is your faith? What evidence demonstrates that you are growing and thriving in your walk with God?

Complacency has no place in a vibrant, wholehearted faith. You can't just drift along, doing the same things the same way day after day and expect to live authentically as a follower of Christ. God's Spirit beckons us to examine ourselves, to make the effort and take the time to look deep within our souls and see what's really going on in there.

Now, I'm not crazy about taking tests. I did fine in school, but exams made me very nervous. Would my brain cooperate under the pressure of having to come up with the right answers? Then there are all those psychological tests that many counselors and employers use. During my discernment for the priesthood, I took a slew of those. I have never quite figured out how they arrive at their conclusions on the basis of the questions they ask, but somehow, they always seemed to nail me. There's no hiding.

And don't get me started on the Episcopal Church's General Ordination Examination I took online as part of the preparation for ordination. That year, all the test-takers experienced a devastating technical glitch that wiped out a whole morning's tense and complicated work.

Social media sites often offer another whole genre of tests that make the circuit from friend to friend. They offer tests to reveal what sort of animal you are, or what your lucky number is, or what your lucky color is, or who your secret friend is. These are kind of fun but silly. And some of them are just pesky efforts to steal your information.

The Spirit of God urges us to take a different kind of examination—a self-test to help us realize that Jesus Christ is in us, that we are solid in the faith. This isn't a pass/fail, heaven/hell type of test. But it does reveal how active and vibrant and wholehearted and authentic our relationship with Christ is at any given moment.

Take some time, regularly, to ask yourself tough questions like these:

✚ Are there disagreements with others I need to sort out in love?

✤ Are there failures to do what the Spirit prompts me to do in reaching out to others?

✤ Have I hurt someone? Neglected something? Missed the mark in obedience to God?

✤ Are my habits holy?

✤ Am I pursuing God's presence through prayer, meditation, and studying the Bible?

✤ Are my priorities in or out of whack? What am I pursuing for self-enjoyment alone?

✤ Am I seeking power to build my own sense of accomplishment?

✤ Am I letting an area of weakness fester without addressing it?

✤ Is my schedule balanced? Am I making room for spiritual activities, serving others, ministering with others, resting, working, playing, enjoying life?

✤ Do I feel I am on a pathway to growth, or am I stalled or meandering in circles?

What other questions do you need to ask in this, the most important test of your life? How would you grade your answers?

The Spirit urges us to do something different if we find we're failing the test. So, what do you need to do?

❧

Holy Spirit, give me firsthand evidence that Jesus Christ is in me. Help me to be sensitive to the state of my relationship with you, examining and considering and weighing my attitudes and actions in light of your will. Help me correct the areas that need your attention. I want to hear you say "well done" when I stand before you. Amen.

3. Blazing with Holiness

> Therefore prepare your minds for action;
> discipline yourselves; set all your hope on the
> grace that Jesus Christ will bring you when he
> is revealed. Like obedient children, do not be
> conformed to the desires that you formerly had
> in ignorance. Instead, as he who called you is
> holy, be holy yourselves in all your conduct; for
> it is written, "You shall be holy, for I am holy."
> —1 PETER 1:13-16

This letter was written centuries ago to believers who faced dark, terrible days of persecution. Most had lost jobs, friends, homes, and possessions. And many would lose their lives. The writer wanted to give them encouragement and instruction. So much was on the line. It was make-or-break time. The apostle knew that these believers could easily slide back into the safety and security of the culture around them, so he urges them, beckons them, to a life of obedience to God, a "way of life shaped by God's life, a life energetic and blazing with holiness" (1 Peter 1:15, *The Message*).

We may not live in the time or place or face the same horrible threats as they did, but we still need to hear the same invitation to holiness. The lure of our society can be so subtle. Before we realize it, we've fallen back into empty old habits. We find ourselves caught in the trap of pursuing wealth or fame or friends or good feelings. We let our spiritual practices slide. We get disconnected from the true, pure, holy power of God. We ignore the calling of the Spirit on our lives.

Before we know it, the self-obsessed culture has swallowed us up again. We feel secure in this dark and hideous emptiness because it's what we came out of. It's familiar. Comfortable. And so many others are there with us.

"Prepare your minds," the Spirit invites us. "Discipline yourselves." Make an intentional effort to be ready to respond to Jesus's call on your life, whatever it may be today. Make it your goal to live "a life energetic and blazing with holiness," a holy life.

What does that mean? What does it mean to be *holy*?

It doesn't mean being better than other people or being exclusively right or specially blessed. It doesn't mean floating blissfully through the world with your mind in the heavenly clouds.

It does mean to be set apart. By God, for God. Prepared and useful for God's purposes. Shining with the light of redemption and righteousness. Energized by the love of God. Devoted to the will of God. Made clean through the presence of the Spirit—our failures removed and replaced by the power and potential of God.

Holiness isn't a feeling; it's a place—a place where God is, a place to which God invites you.

How holy do you feel right now? How does it make you feel when you read God's invitation to you to be holy, as God is holy?

A little inadequate? Slightly fraudulent? Totally incapable?

That's a good place to be. Because that means you know you can't be holy on your own. You are ready for God to use you.

❧

Holy Spirit, I plead for your holy energy, your holy light blazing within me and through me. Peel away the scabs on my soul that keep that from happening. Cleanse me, sharpen me, shape me into the way of life shaped by God's life. Then use me for God's glory. Amen.

4. A Quiet Yes

> Submit yourselves therefore to God. Draw near
> to God, and he will draw near to you. Humble
> yourselves before the Lord, and he will exalt
> you. —James 4:7a, 8a, 10

❦

Enough playing around.

That's it for going through the motions.

Say goodbye to flirting around the edges.

It's time to get real. To make a decision. To get serious about
who you are and how you live in the commonwealth of God.

Will you respond to God's gracious invitations, or will you
keep messing around with half-hearted attitudes, unhealthy
behaviors, unwise choices, and meaningless activities?

The Spirit urges you to submit yourself to God. That means
saying "no" to some things and saying "yes" to God. It means
surrendering your soul to the loving care of the Spirit who
woos you patiently. It means getting serious about your
inner life, your spiritual disciplines of prayer and study and
meditation. It means focusing on your own ministry, how

you can serve others—uniquely, creatively, meaningfully, personally—in Jesus's name. It means making the effort to intentionally draw close to God, who is so ready to welcome you in the divine embrace.

If it means you've hit bottom, welcome to the elevator going up. If it means you have to weep for stupid choices and lazy indifference, go ahead and cry your eyes out. Then wash your face.

You're through playing around. It's time to get serious.

It's time to get down on your knees. You'll meet God there, that's a promise.

Say a quiet yes to God. Then get on your feet and go forth into the world to love and serve the Lord.

Thanks be to God.

⬥

Holy Spirit, I confess my half-heartedness, my laziness, my indifference, my indecisiveness. I say "no" to all that. I say "yes" to you. Let me hear your voice above all the chaos of this world, all the emptiness of my life. Help me get on my feet and follow you. Wherever. Amen.

The Spirit Beckons You to Be Empowered

5. Conformed or Transformed?

> Do not be conformed to this world, but be transformed by the renewing of your minds, so that you may discern what is the will of God—what is good and acceptable and perfect.
> —ROMANS 12:2

God beckons us to stand out in the world. To act authentically. To be ourselves as God made us.

This may not happen automatically. In fact, our tendency is to simply slide into the culture around us, living like anyone else in pursuit of a paycheck or self-gratification or satisfaction at whatever cost.

God's invitation to not conform to this world doesn't mean we all need to move into monasteries or caves in the wilderness. But there's something that happens to us internally when the Spirit of God dwells within us and has free rein over us. People can see a difference in our eyes. In our face. In our responses. In our actions. In our touch. In our embrace.

God has changed us from the inside out.

God wants to develop a maturity in us in which love, joy, peace, kindness, patience, gentleness, goodness, and humility—the fruits of the Spirit—characterize what we think, say, and do. Each of us faces a choice every day: to give in to a culture that seems determined to drag us down to its level of vacuous immaturity—a level that seems to be dropping day by day—or to live in constant, open response to God, who gives us the power to strive for the good and acceptable and perfect.

You already know what it feels like to live responsively to God's desire for you because it's happened before. You take an open, freeing, enthusiastic approach to life. Sensitive to those divine opportunities to reach out to someone in need. Courageous to live a holy life no matter what anyone may think. Lavish in sharing God's limitless love. Sustained through it all by God's powerful presence.

Living like that is the closest thing to heaven on earth. So, why don't we experience that way of life more consistently? God longs for us to live a holy life, no matter what anyone else may think.

If you want to stand apart from others in our damaged, empty culture, fix your attention on God. Ask—and allow—the Spirit to change you from the inside out. Our world might call you crazy. God would call you wise.

⮎⮌

Holy Spirit, I'm tired of being trapped by my fears of being different. Help me fix my attention on God and live so that I can respond readily to God's invitations to live and serve as a mature follower of Christ, even if the world thinks it's crazy. Amen.

6. Fueled and Aflame

Do not lag in zeal, be ardent in spirit, serve the
Lord. Rejoice in hope, be patient in suffering,
persevere in prayer. —ROMANS 12:11-12

⌖

Many years ago, I burned out. I hit a wall. I "lagged in zeal."
The work I was doing was meaningful, and my colleagues
were marvelous. But I reached a point where it wasn't working
for me. The heavy, stressful, and growing responsibilities kept
me exhausted and unable to connect with loved ones—and
with God.

Finally, I gave out. The problems and frustrations and
disconnects I experienced in my job were beginning to affect
my very faith. Was I really serving God? Was God the kind of
God who would require such grueling service "for the cause"?

I believe God was using that situation to call me to move
on—not only to a different place of work but to a different
place in my faith. The door suddenly opened wide for another
opportunity, one that challenged and blessed me for many
years. In fact, on the very day I decided I had had enough, the
phone rang with an offer to accept this new opportunity, one
that challenged and blessed me for many years.

In the end, I believe I gained some maturity and grew in my understanding of my calling and in the authenticity of my faith—which I'm not sure would have ever happened if I had not tried something new. Yes, it took some time to lick my wounds and rebuild my faith and learn to serve God freely and willingly and lovingly again. But I moved on.

Burnout challenged my faith, but my wrestling and questioning helped me grow and mature in my understanding of my calling. Doubt deepened my faith.

Now, years later, I find myself in serving another religious organization, wanting to give all of myself to managing it effectively and reaching people through its work. And the Spirit's warning here is fresh to me. The last thing I want to do is burn out—again. Yes, I want to live full force for God, responsive to the Spirit's guidance, cleansed in the crucible of real faith. But it is so easy to focus on all the responsibilities, the needs, the opportunities—and run out of spiritual gas.

"Don't burn out," Eugene Peterson recasts this verse from Romans. "Keep yourselves fueled and aflame."

The key, this passage indicates, is to maintain a living, alert, cheerful, empowered relationship with God. We need to understand that, as the saying goes, "There is a God, and you're not God." *You are not God. God is God.* Such simple, humble awareness keeps us from working out of our own strength and wisdom rather than God's.

So let's keep fueled and aflame in God's power. The only way to do this is to keep in touch with God—authentically and faithfully. We can't just go through the motions of attending worship services, reading devotional books, and praying the usual prayers, but rather we must be intentional about maintaining the connection: taking time to meditate on God's word, praying honestly and frequently, and serving others genuinely, spontaneously, and meaningfully.

When circumstances bite you and the going gets tough, don't give up. Expect that you will have times like that, and roll with them. Stay connected to God—but also be sensitive to those times when God may be calling you to move on.

Simple advice. The apostle makes it sound so simple anyway, but for many of us, it's a lifelong challenge, often difficult to practice because we think we know so much better than God. It's not easy to give up our self-assured, self-confident, prideful attitudes and be expectant, empowered, alert servants of the Master.

I'm going to work on that today. You?

Holy Spirit, there is a fine line between doing right things in my power and in God's. One leads to self-destruction and burnout. The other brings cheerful energy and fulfillment. I know which path I want to follow. Give me the discernment I need to keep following it, realizing when I wander off in my own power. Fuel me with your presence so I can keep burning for you without burning out. Amen.

7. Getting the Best of Evil

Do not be overcome by evil, but overcome evil
with good. —Romans 12:21

❧

Good versus evil. So much of popular culture revolves
around this theme. It's a primal foundation on which all of
life plays out.

When I was a boy, the battle of good versus evil absorbed a
large part of my consciousness. I read story after story about
heroes of all kinds battling for truth and justice in comic
books and adventure stories.

It was all so simple. You knew precisely who the good guys
were and who the evil guys were. You knew who to root
for. You could count on the heroes to behave in exactly the
same ways from battle to battle. And you knew who would
ultimately win.

There's Superman, who came from beyond with the power to
save humanity, and whose early comic-strip adventures stressed
overcoming the oppression of the poor and downtrodden
with righteous justice. And Spider-Man, whose powerful

motto, "With great power there must also come—great responsibility!"—stated in his very first appearance in *Amazing Fantasy #15*—is a virtual paraphrase of Luke 12:48, "From everyone to whom much has been given, much will be required; and from the one to whom much has been entrusted, even more will be demanded."

While thinking about all this I ran across a fascinating bit of dialogue by the inimitable Stan Lee in *Captain America #105*. Our flag-waving hero becomes an evangelist as he battles the French villain Batroc while a deadly bomb ticks away:

> *Cap*: "Now out of my way, mister! I'm gonna try to reach it…and de-fuse it…or die trying!"
>
> *Batroc*: "Die! Zat is a most unpleasant word!… My so-great speed will take me to safety…while you stupidly risk your life for zee undeserving masses!"
>
> *Cap*: "There was another who gave his life for the masses…many centuries ago… And though he was the wisest one of all…he never thought of the humblest living being…as undeserving!"

It's clear that bad guys generally have a hopeless opinion of humanity and are out only to save their own butts, and maybe make some money and oppress some people in the process. Captain America, on the other hand, embodies the religious ideals of truth, justice, self-sacrifice, altruism, and hope.

I find such good-guy certainty comforting. How I wish life were like that—we would know how it's all going to end and know which side to pick to be on the winning team.

Paul seems to draw similar distinctions in his letters to the Christians at Rome. We are in a battle, he writes—a battle with eternal consequences. As believers, we are on the side of good, but we must wrestle with evil continually in all shapes and sizes and ways. But sometimes life doesn't seem so easily divided. We yearn for sharp clarity, but all we see are shades of gray. Issues that divide political parties, denominations, churches, and even families are rarely simple yes-or-no decisions.

Some behaviors can easily be labeled evil. But while battle lines are drawn over many issues, with each side convinced they are the right and good side, we might instead step back and see a more complex picture.

This approach can be frustrating. But it also stretches our hearts and minds to work through and discuss and consider and pray over and work on.

There may not be a whole lot that you and I can do to solve some of these burning issues of our day, at least not right now, so let's consider this scriptural admonition on a personal level.

The Spirit urges us to stand strong in the face of injustice or hatred in our own lives and, like those altruistic superheroes, do good. Do mercy. Do justice. Do peace.

What would that look like in your own sphere of life? How can you do good and not evil in the life of your fellow workers, your neighbors, your family, your country? How can you do good and not evil in the face of unfairness or need or pain or sickness or oppression?

You and I aren't superheroes in a comic book story, battling the cosmic forces of evil. But we are engaged in a spiritual struggle of life and death, of light and darkness. We are part of the multitude of those who choose to live in the way of love, God's way, striving to do good in a world struggling desperately to make sense out of the chaos and to experience love in the midst of need and emptiness. We can be do-gooders in the best sense of the word. Every simple act of kindness, every small step we take to offer positive, God-directed help and guidance, shared in the spirit of Christ with someone in need, helps to overcome evil.

Someday, in some way, there may be some sort of unfathomable cosmic, spiritual battle between the forces of good and the forces of evil, when good will win, unalterably, eternally, decisively. In the meantime, light a candle in the darkness today through an act of outrageous good. Then light two tomorrow. And the next day. And the next. Overcome evil with good.

≈

Holy Spirit, it's so easy to focus on the wrong done to me, the ways the world mistreats me and messes up my life. That, I realize, is letting evil overcome me. It holds me down and keeps me focused on the wrong things. You call me to step forward and share your light by doing good. Help me to do that today. Open my eyes and my heart to the many opportunities I will come across to overcome evil. Amen.

8. Stand Firm in Strength

> Be strong in the Lord and in the strength of his
> power. Put on the whole armor of God, so that
> you may be able to stand against the wiles of
> the devil. —EPHESIANS 6:10-11

Oh, how we yearn for more strength—physical, emotional,
spiritual strength. How we beg God for health and wisdom to
live as God's people in this mean, conniving world.

But the Spirit beckons us to acknowledge that God has already
generously set a place before us with everything we need for
strength and protection and health. Yet God never forces
anything on us—we must take up these resources for ourselves.
We must put our spiritual armory to use. We must "be strong
in the Lord and in the strength of his power."

"Stand therefore, and fasten the belt of truth around your
waist, and put on the breastplate of righteousness," Paul
continues (Ephesians 6:14). Or, as Eugene Peterson puts it in
The Message: "Truth, righteousness, peace, faith, and salvation
are more than words. Learn how to apply them. You'll need
them throughout your life."

The Spirit encourages us to learn how to apply these powerful spiritual resources to work in our lives. When we do, we're protected as though covered by solid armor. Nothing can get through to wound us. Nothing can bring us to defeat.

Take some time to meditate on what these words mean to you, how they can become more real to you every day:

+ *Truth* is the *word of God,* revealed to us through our relationship to God and the indwelling of the Spirit. We sit at Jesus's feet, breathing in God's truth through scripture, trusting God to reveal whatever we need to know whenever we need to know it. Trusting in the authenticity of God protects us from what's false and empty and unreal. *How will you embrace truth in your life?*

+ *Righteousness* is the *way of God.* As children of God we are clothed, covered, healed by the righteousness of Christ, who invites us to live fruitful, energetic lives as God's servants. Living in righteousness protects us from falling into patterns that can be destructive to ourselves or others. *How will you embrace righteousness in your life?*

+ *Peace is the presence of God.* The Spirit infuses us with the balm of God's peace when we are open to walking in God's way. Living in peace protects us from the world's chaos and dissonance. *How will you embrace peace in your life?*

✦ *Faith is the life of God.* The Spirit welcomes us to trust, to know, to rest, to live in the reality of Christ, seeking God's presence through prayer and understanding. Living in faith protects us from wandering from our true calling as a child of God into meaningless, empty pursuits. *How will you embrace faith in your life?*

✦ *Salvation is the promise of God.* The Spirit heals our wounded souls, fills in our empty spaces, and leads us into eternal life through Christ. And as we heal, we are called to share this salvation with others. Living in salvation protects us from living for our own selves, which leads only to hell in every sense of the word. *How will you embrace salvation in your life?*

Truth. Righteousness. Peace. Faith. Salvation. God offers powerful resources for each of us—resources we'll need throughout our life. Will you put them on like pieces of protective armor today? And tomorrow?

After all, "Our struggle is not against enemies of blood and flesh, but against the rulers, against the authorities, against the cosmic powers of this present darkness, against the spiritual forces of evil in the heavenly places" (Ephesians 6:12).

Holy Spirit, you have given me a spiritual armory, all the resources I need to make my way through this world and into your commonwealth. Give me the wisdom and strength to take them up and put them to good use, for the glory of God. Amen.

The Spirit Beckons You to Reach Out

9. Repairing Broken People

> My friends, if anyone is detected in a
> transgression, you who have received the
> Spirit should restore such a one in a spirit
> of gentleness. Take care that you yourselves
> are not tempted. —GALATIANS 6:1

Here's how we typically treat someone we know who fails
morally: We judge them. Criticize them. Gossip about them.
Dismiss them. Abandon them. Ignore them. Shame them.
Punish them. Ostracize them. Give up on them.

The Spirit of God calls us to do something entirely different:
"Restore such a one in a spirit of gentleness." This is part of
living creatively in the Spirit.

Paul doesn't describe what transgression this is—large or small. That doesn't matter. It's about someone who has fallen, drifted away into unhealthy patterns or actions or temptations. We are to lovingly, forgivingly restore such a one. What does that mean?

Strong's Concordance defines the Greek word translated restore this way: to complete thoroughly, to repair, adjust, fit, mend, make perfect, perfectly join together.

Someone who has fallen apart spiritually needs to be made whole again—completed and repaired, mended, lovingly put back together. This can be realized through counseling, meaningful support, prayer, and even just being present with the person through whatever difficult situation they find themselves in.

Sometimes it works, sometimes it doesn't.

Many years ago, a friend of mine from the church I was attending at the time went through some sort of midlife crisis. He bought a sporty, two-seater convertible, even though his wife was pregnant with their second child. Before long, even more desperate cries of the midlife male could be heard. He told me glowingly about his new assistant at work, a beautiful and vibrant young woman, and how excited he was to have her working with him. My spiritual spider-sense went off, but I didn't say anything.

A few weeks later, he called to say he wanted to talk with me. During a Sunday morning church service, we stepped outside and while we walked among the tombstones of the faithful of the past, he unfolded in thrilled tones how God had finally brought the perfect woman into his life—his new assistant.

I was the first person he had revealed this situation to. I suspect he thought that I, who he knew casually for several years as a good, friendly, open-minded, supportive pal, would encourage his newfound freedom and "God-given" love.

I listened to him quietly for nearly half an hour. While his wife was at home with their young child, and only weeks away from giving birth to a second, he had been dining out with this "passionate, creative" woman. They had spent a good bit of time together, talking, sharing, spinning dreams.

It was clear to him that God was giving him a gift—a woman who more closely shared his life goals, who looked and acted and fulfilled his dream of a companion. Besides, his wife had all these other problems: he never quite fit into her family, she didn't really understand him, etc. Now God was answering his prayers for a relationship that would be so much better than his current marriage. At least he fervently thought so.

Finally, he turned to me with an expectant look, as though inviting my understanding and encouragement to "accept God's gift."

I said simply, "Run. Run as fast as you can away from this situation. This is nothing but trouble. You have a wife and two children, and you are about to destroy everybody's lives with one wrong-headed decision."

Perhaps I was harsh. Maybe I was not as loving and forgiving as this passage calls for. But I truly said it out of love for him.

He was shocked and deeply hurt. So, he said with a touch of bitterness, I didn't understand him after all. I was just like everybody else—judgmental and close-minded. I assured him of my love and concern for him, but I also wanted to protect him and his family from the painful consequences of bad choices. I encouraged him to at least work through his issues with his wife in therapy.

Ultimately, this man was surrounded and mentored by several wise people. It was a long and painful process, but after some months he made the decision to stay with his wife and children.

So, I suppose this invitation works, whether or not you get it exactly right.

The truth is, this story could easily be told the other way around, with me trying to convince a friend that some wayward desire I had must be God's will. We all have much to learn from one another.

But here's the point: if a body of believers is willing to stick with someone flailing against God's will and love them, counsel them, speak truth to them, and forgive them, then hearts will soften. Stubborn wills will relent. Lives will be restored.

When you live creatively in a spirit of love and forgiveness, broken people can be repaired. And, by the way, there's an imperative here to "take care." Because, who knows, someday that broken person might be you.

Holy Spirit, melt my heart with the fire of your holy, forgiving love, so that I will be prepared to minister to broken hearts and shattered souls. Thank you that you have created a family of faith to surround me in those times, to keep me in touch with you even when I feel like running away. Amen.

10. Stooping Down

> Bear one another's burdens, and in this way you
> will fulfill the law of Christ. —GALATIANS 6:2

We are all in this thing together. We need each other. We all
have burdens to share. This is how we make it through.

It's easy to think about carrying others' burdens when it
involves your close friends or family members or even fellow
church members. It's a bit harder to stretch the boundaries of
our comfort zone beyond those safe circles.

Working in an urban setting was a new experience for me
when I began my ministry with *Day 1* more than twenty years
ago at our then-new offices and recording studio in Midtown
Atlanta. Our facility was on the campus of All Saints'
Episcopal Church, which has long offered effective outreach
services to those in need in the community, on their own and
in concert with other area churches. Because of their presence
in an urban center, I routinely encountered people begging for
money. Often, they would carry plaintive requests scrawled on
pieces of cardboard.

I didn't know exactly what to do regarding dealing with requests like that. I've heard conflicting advice from well-meaning people. For a while, I always carried a few dollar bills in my pocket to give to whoever asked me for money. After all, someone once told me, our responsibility is to be willing to give—it is the recipient's responsibility to decide whether to spend it wisely or otherwise.

Whenever I walked in the neighborhood or sat at a red light in my car while street people walked alongside staring helplessly and holding a cup out, I would hand over a dollar bill or two. I'd also often ask their name and chat just a minute.

One time, some folks at the office were talking about a particular homeless man who'd been harassing them outside the parking deck. I blurted out, "Oh, you mean Ray?" They looked at me in surprise: I knew his name? He really wasn't a bad sort, though he could be a bit aggressive.

Of course, others I've talked to who have worked specifically in ministry to homeless people have warned me against giving such folks anything. They only use that money for harmful stuff, they say, and you don't need to encourage that. There are enough other programs to feed and house them temporarily that you can steer them to, they say.

Sometimes I do that, encouraging someone who approaches me to walk a few blocks to the assistance center operated by a coalition of churches and groups. I've also bought a bunch of fast-food gift cards that I give away to anyone who is hungry.

Every so often, far too rarely, I stop and talk with someone barely surviving on the street. Their stories vary wildly, and some evidently need mental health care. But what do I do? Is that enough? Is it enough to give an occasional gift to an organization that serves the needs of the oppressed? Shouldn't I be down there ladling soup?

This is a conversation I have frequently with God. I want to reach out and share others' burdens, but I want to do it wisely and helpfully in ways that make sense and help in effective ways. And I want to do this as part of the body of Christ.

I want to remain open to the Spirit's beckoning to me in order to complete Christ's law of love. How do I do this well? And will you join me in this?

❧

Holy Spirit, the oppressed come in many colors, from all social levels and economic strata. Oppression is the universal condition of the heart. Help me be part of the embrace of God's Spirit in the world to reach out to those who are hurting in wise, effective ways. Help me to obey the law of Christ to love God and to love one another. Amen.

11. Putting On Love

> As God's chosen ones, holy and beloved, clothe
> yourselves with compassion, kindness, humility,
> meekness, and patience....Above all, clothe
> yourselves with love, which binds everything
> together in perfect harmony.
> —COLOSSIANS 3:12,14

⬿⬷

I don't think my closet holds a very impressive wardrobe. It's standard stuff. Some consignment store acquisitions, a few shirts and pants from online sales, and plenty of clothes I've had for more than a decade. Or two.

However, I do have several impressive suits. One of them is even a tuxedo.

For eleven years, I'd been working as senior copywriter at an advertising agency, where we observed "casual Friday" every day of the week—jeans, or even shorts, and a polo shirt would do. Only rarely, when we had new clients to impress, did we dress in anything approaching a coat and tie.

When I became the president of an organization, I felt I had to change my ways. I owned two or three suits that almost fit me—maybe the slacks were a bit too tight around the middle or the coat sleeves just a tad too long.

I needed a wardrobe makeover. But no reality show would have me.

One day, I shared my quandary with a friend over coffee at our favorite cafe. "Oh, I can help you there," he said. "I've got something like two dozen really nice, tailored suits my boss gave me—he's worn them a few times and just keeps buying new ones. I'll be glad to give you some of those. They should fit you pretty well."

I looked at him in disbelief—he would *give* me a bunch of suits? And expensive ones at that?

It turned out he also had a handful of ties he never wore. He had never gotten the suits altered to fit his size. And his own office was becoming more dress-casual, so he rarely wore suits anymore anyway.

I ended up with several thousand dollars' worth of quality menswear in my closet because my friend cared. Even better, those suits and pants fit me to an absolute T—no alterations required.

I think of my closet as I read this passage. These days I usually dress more casually, but it does feel good to wear a well-tailored suit sometimes.

My friend did for me in a physical sense what God does for us all in a spiritual sense. The apostle writes that God has picked out a wonderful and priceless wardrobe for each of us. But they aren't designer label suits. They are of far more worth.

It's a wardrobe of *compassion, kindness, humility, meekness, and patience.*

We are to put on those traits like a garment, covering ourselves from head to toe. Living abundantly requires clothing ourselves in those character qualities like a garment.

But no matter what else we put on, there's one spiritual garment that's mandatory: love.

When I get dressed in the morning, thinking about the day ahead and its many and varied responsibilities, I try to keep this holy imperative in mind. As I pull on my pants, button my shirt, and don my coat, I imagine myself putting on compassion, kindness, humility, meekness, and patience, and love.

Our lives, our words, our actions are to radiate these qualities with everyone we meet. It's as if the Holy Spirit dwelling within us permeates through our skin into the world around us, touching everyone we meet.

Let's not go out into the world naked. God has provided an exquisite wardrobe chosen expressly for each of us. Dress well.

Holy Spirit, may you be a fragrant aroma of love around me today. Clothe me, cover me, so that all who I meet today will sense your presence, receive your compassion and kindness, and know your love. Amen.

12. What to Do with What You Hear

Be doers of the word, and not merely hearers
who deceive themselves. —JAMES 1:22

⤙❧⤚

If only the church would take up the challenging imperative
of this verse: not just to *hear* the word but to *be doers* of the
word. To act on it, live it out, put it to work—just *do* it. It
would revolutionize the world.

No charges of hypocrisy could be lodged against the church—
preaching one thing and doing another. No shunning or even
ostracizing those whom scripture urges the church to welcome
and serve.

I'm sure you agree with me. The only problem is, of course,
that the church is made up of individual human beings like
you and me.

So, it starts with us. As I read this passage, I can identify
uncomfortably with it: "For if any are hearers of the word
and not doers, they are like those who look at themselves
in a mirror; for they look at themselves and, on going away,
immediately forget what they were like" (James 1:23-24).

We're scatterbrained. Distracted. We can research and study and argue the fine points of the Bible text then walk away and act as if we had never even read it.

I once heard a story, possibly apocryphal but unfortunately not necessarily so, about a homeless family—a woman and three children under the age of 10—who approached a church one cold late autumn evening, having seen lights on in the fellowship hall.

The mother knocked on the kitchen door seeking food or any sort of help. No one answered the door. They knocked again. Still no response. The woman peered into one of the windows not far from the kitchen door and saw a group of about a dozen people around a table, with a man standing near them talking and gesturing. There were people there. Didn't they hear her?

She knocked on the window. She saw heads turn in her direction, most of them bearing scowls. She waved at the people gathered in the warm fellowship hall. Finally, the man walked to the door. She anticipated warm support, maybe some covered dish leftovers for her children.

The door opened, the man stuck his head out, surveyed the scene, and said, "We're busy with Bible study. Come back tomorrow." And he shut the door.

The mother was surprised and saddened—and also alarmed, as the temperature was dropping rapidly. She tried knocking a few more times, but the people kept their noses in their Bibles. So she huddled her three children together to wait out the cold night in a back corner of the parking lot, since the man had said to come back the next day. She had nowhere else to go.

Tragically, the temperatures dropped so low that night that her youngest child, a little girl, contracted pneumonia. She died soon after.

Thank God, that church was punched in the gut so forcefully by the needless tragedy they could have averted that they changed their ways. They began acting on what they were studying, and soon after launched a ministry to the homeless called "Annie's Kitchen" in memory of, and named for, the little girl who died because of their negligence.

Not a day goes by, the story goes, that those believers don't mourn for the little girl. But they are doing what they can to redeem the tragic loss.

God help us if we neglect the *doing* of the divine admonitions of reaching out to the poor and needy because we're so busily involved in just doing "church."

Where God beckons, follow. Here's why: "Those who look into the perfect law, the law of liberty, and persevere, being not hearers who forget but doers who act—they will be blessed in their doing" (James 1:25).

No more letting what we hear from God's word go in one ear, echo around in our brain for a moment, and leave through the other ear, leaving no trace behind.

No more missing the blessing.

What is God showing you? Do it. Act on it. Stick with it. And experience the delight and affirmation of your empowering Lord.

❧

Holy Spirit, your word is within me. Make it burn. Grab hold of my stubborn will and soften it so that I will be open to every opportunity for obedience. I want to delight my God with a loving heart. Give me the power, strength, and wisdom to make that happen. Amen.

13. The Glory of Humility

> All of you must clothe yourselves with humility
> in your dealings with one another, for "God
> opposes the proud, but gives grace to the
> humble." Humble yourselves therefore under
> the mighty hand of God, so that he may exalt
> you in due time. —1 PETER 5:5B-6

When someone asks you to work in the nursery or to come
out for a workday at church or to serve on a committee or
board, do you immediately think to yourself, *What's in it for
me? Will this make me look good? How can I use this to my own
advantage?*

When you make a sale or have a successful business encounter,
are you tempted to think, *I am so good. My sales are higher than
anyone else's. I'm clearly the most important salesperson in this
company.*

When someone asks a question about something you think is
obvious or makes a statement you disagree with, do you think,
What an idiot. How can that person believe that?

Most of us are guilty of such thoughts at one time or another. But such reactions reflect arrogance and pride, qualities that keep us closed, unyielding, and distant from others and God.

We live in a culture addicted to status. Self-promotion has become valued far more than self-discipline. People outdo each other to become a bigger social media influencer with ever-increasing numbers of followers. "Me first" is the primary attitude on which most people build their lives.

Humility is indeed a lost art.

What's in it for me? How can I use this to my advantage? Those are the questions, spoken or not, that so often lurk in one's mind whenever a situation arises that requires a personal response. It's a knee-jerk reaction to opportunities of service and love that stifles the attitude God calls us to wear: humility.

Take a minute to put it on. Consciously clothe yourself with it. Let it surround you, cover you, embrace you. The Spirit urges you to wear it.

That's what Jesus does. He sets aside everything he is, every divine perk he possesses, to serve God. To become one of us. At the cost of his life.

Even though the cost of humility for us is not nearly so high, it can still cost us, at least in the world's eyes. We may lose prestige, privilege, or some earthly authority. But we gain a pure heart, a clean conscious, and God's pleasure.

You see, humility may not get you ahead in society, but it is the only way to enter the presence of God. It envelops us in God's purpose and keeps us quiet and patient, even when the world explodes around us. It lifts us into the clean, clear heavenly atmosphere. It leads to all sorts of unique blessings, as God promises throughout scripture:

The humble are as contented as a baby in a mother's arms (see Psalm 131:2)

The humble avoid conflict and discord (see Proverbs 13:10)

The humble experience the presence of the Lord (see Isaiah 57:15)

The humble will be lifted up before all (see Luke 14:11)

The humble will become the greatest in God's kingdom (see Matthew 18:4)

The humble will experience God's pure, powerful grace (see James 4:6)

The humble will receive the highest and best honors (see Proverbs 18:12)

And those are just a few of the promises.

One of the greatest paradoxes of the Christian faith is that humility is the avenue to glory. Eventually.

In the meantime, turn your eyes and your heart from yourself to your neighbor. And put yourself humbly under the hand of God. It is a mighty, loving, secure, and comforting embrace. And it is the way to an inexpressible glory.

⁂

Holy Spirit, I place my soul, my heart, my life into the hands of my loving, mighty God. Work on my pride—I know the process can be painful, but it is purifying. Thank you that God is willing to work with me on this. Amen.

The Spirit Beckons You to Peace

14. Blessed Enemies

> Bless those who persecute you; bless and do not curse them. —ROMANS 12:14

The apostle isn't suggesting anything novel here. In his extensive list of ways believers should love others in his letter to the Romans, he is simply restating one of Jesus's most radical teachings:

"But I say to you, Love your enemies and pray for those who persecute you" (Matthew 5:44).

All of us deeply agree with this goal—in principle, anyway. What's tough is when we have to live it out. Then it suddenly makes no sense. And it's impossible, it seems, to practice.

What would happen if this attitude were practiced in one of the world's many hotspots? Or between Democrats and Republicans and Independents? Liberals and conservatives from one extreme to the other? Baptists and Episcopalians? Queers and straights? Young and old? Blacks and Whites and Browns? Young and old? Brothers and sisters and siblings? Husbands and wives, partners and spouses? Neighbors? Co-workers? Competitors?

What would happen? Our world would turn on its head if even a few people truly accepted this invitation to radical love and peace.

As we've seen, the problem is that we're all full of pride. And blessing enemies requires great amounts of humility.

Books have been written to help people understand how to do this without losing themselves, becoming doormats or being codependent. Sometimes it seems all that advice simply helps us get around this command without feeling guilty.

I'm certainly not saying I have this one nailed down. But I do enjoy surprising people who are angry with me with a little understanding, acceptance, and friendliness.

Sometimes I'm surprised at the angry (often unsigned) emails or voicemails we get at the *Day 1* radio program/podcast—from all sides. For instance, we'll hear from people angry that we have women preachers on our program and people angry that we don't have enough women or people of color. We work on that balance of diversity constantly.

Not long after I started producing the radio program, I became concerned that our program sounded dated. What little music we used was very simple, just a piano and flute, performing "A Mighty Fortress Is Our God."

I called our list of radio station affiliates to see what they thought of the program and find out how we might serve them more effectively. A number of program directors (most of them at secular stations representing all sorts of music and spoken formats) said that, while our program was well produced and presented a much-needed positive message, the music and format didn't fit well within their station's image. They wanted a more contemporary, appealing sound so listeners wouldn't tune out.

So, we worked with a local composer with numerous television, movie, and commercial credits, who created a new palette of music for our program—theme songs and music beds. He came up with the idea of using an old tune used in nearly all our participating denominations, the *Old One Hundredth* (the tune to one often-sung version of the Doxology), as the basis for our new theme song. But he scored it with strong percussion, contemporary keyboards, and even an electric guitar.

Oh, it was different all right. I thought it was beautiful, capturing the meaningful, upbeat, contemporary feel we were aiming for but still using a beloved church tune.

You might imagine the phone calls, letters, and emails I received from some of our most faithful listeners, upset by the change after so many years. The truth is, we received fewer complaints than I anticipated—I think most of our listeners were ready for the change, too. But those I did receive were rather heated.

I responded to each one in as friendly and understanding a way as I could. When I explained that many of the radio station program directors said they would have no choice but to cancel the program if it wasn't more up-to-date sounding, they began to understand. The more we interacted, the more positive they became. Though they may never grow to like our theme song or background music, they could see why we made the change. And they became even stronger supporters of our efforts to provide inspiration for the real world.

I could have written these people off, muttering curses under my breath. But I tried to understand where they were coming from. After all, if they didn't care about the program, they wouldn't have communicated their feelings so strongly. I've found time and again that engaging with such folks warmly and patiently while explaining my thoughts clearly and honestly seems to magically reduce the anger and tension.

That's a simple example, I admit. But if I can just multiply that practice in my life, maybe I can grow closer to accepting this divine invitation to make peace with everyone I meet.

Life offers more than enough opportunities to do just that every day.

Holy Spirit, there are more than enough people in my life with whom I can practice this principle of peacemaking. The truth is, I really don't want to love my enemies. They deserve my scorn, my muttered curses. Yet you call me to something different. A new way to live. A way of love. I can't do it without you. Amen.

15. Working It Out

> Work out your own salvation with fear and
> trembling; for it is God who is at work in you,
> enabling you both to will and to work for his
> good pleasure. —Philippians 2:12b-13

꧁꧂

It is so easy to let life wipe you out. Obliterate every bit of
peace left within you. Load the weight of daily responsibilities,
the crush of strained relationships, the burden of dashed
expectations onto your soul.

Life certainly takes a toll. Every day.

As I write this, I think of the major stresses revolving around
my heart and mind that are weighing me down. And these are
on top of the two or three dozen everyday hassles of life and
the challenges facing our community and world.

The burdens involve:

✚ A major decision my spouse and I are considering
(Is now the time? Should we do it? Are we being
wise? Will we be able to handle it financially?).

✛ A deeply disturbing situation erupting in the life of a couple I'm close to (Will they make it? How can I help? What should they do?).

✛ Preparing for important meetings regarding the future direction of our ministry (Can we find needed new funding sources? Will we be able to move forward in effective, creative ways? Will I have smart ideas and the ability to bring them to reality?).

✛ And the desire to write something today that connects with you and your life situation—and provides some hope and encouragement (Will I be able to be honest yet helpful? Can I bring God's truth to your life situation? Will I make my deadline?).

It's tiring. Overwhelming at times. Sometimes I feel like I need to crawl into bed and just sleep for a week or two to catch up with my need for peace and rest. Maybe you can identify. If not today, you might tomorrow.

But something amazing happens when I listen to the voice of the Spirit beckoning me to more: "Redouble your efforts. Be energetic in your life of salvation, reverent and sensitive before God" (Philippians 2:12, *The Message*).

When I stand up and reach out and make a fresh effort, somehow God fills me with the energy I need. The creativity I crave. The sensitivity to others' needs I hope for. The desire to do my best to be a servant of Christ to others I encounter.

Don't let this come across as though God wants to squeeze every ounce of energy out of you. That's not the deal here. It's rather about filling you with peace, purpose, and fulfillment, along with the spiritual power to make it so. It's about helping you realize God's calling on your life in exciting, invigorating ways. When that happens, the tiredness washes away. The heaviness lifts—at least for a while—as you focus on other needs and opportunities. God's energy works in and through you to fulfill God's will for you.

When you open yourself back up to energetic service, it gives God pleasure. It also gives you peace. And joy. And hope for the next time you find yourself worn out beyond all measure.

⚬⚬⚬

Holy Spirit, when I find myself in need of peace, remind me to ask for it. To seek divine energy. To remember this verse's promise. I want to sense you working within me, empowering me to serve. I want to give God pleasure through my obedient, sensitive, reverent, and energetic heart. Amen.

16. Request Line

> Do not worry about anything, but in
> everything by prayer and supplication with
> thanksgiving let your requests be made known
> to God. And the peace of God, which surpasses
> all understanding, will guard your hearts and
> your minds in Christ Jesus. —PHILIPPIANS 4:6-7

It's amazing how busy the mind can keep itself in the
middle of the night, while the body is lying there wide
awake. One after another, life's concerns and worries arise,
demand attention, and tumble around the brain cells,
causing adrenaline to rush in fear, which wakes us up further,
which opens the door of our minds to still more concerns
and worries—including the fact that we aren't getting
enough sleep.

God's Spirit beckons us to stop fretting. Instead of worrying,
we are invited to pray.

There can be a mighty fine line, however, between worrying
over something and praying for something. I know how easy

it is to begin praying for my concerns only to forget who I'm talking to and get mired in my angst once again.

Sometimes I can't specifically review my concerns in prayer—it only makes me more anxious thinking about them all. In those cases, I often turn to meditative, repetitive prayer, such as the Jesus Prayer: *Lord Jesus Christ, have mercy on me.* Or the Lord's Prayer. Or even the Hail Mary. A memorized prayer forces me to engage my mind and my heart, to focus on God instead of my fears and worries.

Other times, I let some psalms or other verses I've memorized wash through my mind, rinse, and repeat. Before long, I find my worries have subsided, and I drift away into peaceful sleep. Sometimes that's the best I can do.

What the Spirit encourages is to turn the concerns over to God. Lift them up to heaven, and then let go. Let Christ himself displace the worries at the core of our life. A wonderful thing happens when we do that. We experience true peace, a peace beyond what our busy brain can conceive, a sense of God's presence and wholeness. We catch a glimpse of God's perfect will, everything coming together for good. We settle down in the realization that God is working in and through every situation that worries us. What we choose to focus on, and how we choose to focus on it, is up to us.

The Spirit beckons us to choose prayer: to choose the pursuit of God's wholeness, to choose Jesus at the center of our life, to choose peace.

❦

Holy Spirit, when my brain goes feverish with worry and fear, pour your cool, calming, peaceful presence over me. Help me focus on Christ, beckoning to me with outstretched arms, waiting for me to place those burdens in his strong hands. Help me to choose to pray. Amen.

The Spirit Beckons You
to Friendship

17. Loving from the Center

> Let love be genuine; hate what is evil, hold fast
> to what is good; love one another with mutual
> affection; outdo one another in showing honor.
> —ROMANS 12:9-10

Sometimes God brings people together in unexpected
ways. Many years ago, I joined an internet discussion group
regarding men's issues. This was in the mid-1990s when the
men's movement had grown rapidly in a variety of ways.

One of the posts on this discussion group immediately
resonated with me because the writer was attempting to tie
his faith in with his need to discover what being a "real man"

today was all about. As it turned out, I couldn't keep up with all the email discussions so I soon unsubscribed. But something about that post stayed with me. So, boldly, I sent an email directly to the writer to pursue some of the points he'd brought up.

At first, he was a bit suspicious—not a bad trait when it comes to dealing with people on the internet. But soon we were corresponding back and forth with regularity. His name was Jim; he was an Episcopal priest in Queens, New York. Very early on, Jim introduced me to another of his regular email correspondents, a Methodist minister in South Africa named Colin. The three of us still correspond by email decades later.

The richness of our email fellowship has been one of the joys of my life. Over the years, we have shared the deepest of pains and the greatest of joys. Colin and Jim are both a few years older than I am and have survived stints on the front lines of life and ministry, so I appreciate their hard-won wisdom.

After a couple of years of corresponding, Jim invited me to his home for a visit. I had never been to New York City before and was excited about the possibility. Of course, you must be very careful of meeting people you run into on the internet— you never know what the truth might be behind the email persona. But Jim and I had developed such an easy and honest rapport that I felt confident all would be fine.

Was that an understatement. That weekend we first met "in real life" it seemed as though we'd known each other for years. At that time, Jim was still serving a parish in Queens in an area that had grown largely Latino/Hispanic. So, he and his amazing wife, June, a college literature professor, learned Spanish; ultimately the eleven o'clock service at his church became the Spanish-language service, welcoming all in the neighborhood, while the nine o'clock service met the needs of the longtime Anglo members who remained faithful to the church. I attended both services the weekend I first visited—and they were as different as night and day. And yet both of them, one traditional, the other much livelier, were marked by God's loving presence.

Jim was a superb host that weekend, taking me around the city to see the sights, making me feel so at home in the huge, strange city. We talked for hours about our faith, our doubts, our growing edges, our hopes, our families and friends.

I was struck immediately by Jim's generosity of spirit, his warm affection, his easy presence, and yes, his genuine love. The wisdom he shared struck home in my heart—and yet it was a guileless wisdom, as though he didn't realize just how wise he was.

Since that first weekend visit many years ago, my spouse and I have been privileged to stay with Jim and June on other weekend getaways and business trips. And he has been to Atlanta a few times over the years as well—even participating in my ordination as an Episcopal priest, which meant the world to me. We only wish, someday, that Colin could join us—or we could go visit him in South Africa.

As I've gotten to know Jim and June over the years, I'm constantly amazed at their holy energy. Jim is retired from the parish ministry now but still keeps busy. For a while, he taught at a community college, and he served as an interim at a Latino/Hispanic church in Washington Heights. And he still fills a pulpit—or an organist's bench—in a church somewhere in the area occasionally.

Jim is also a student of Brazilian jiu-jitsu, even in his eighth decade of life. He's been deeply involved in ministry to the homeless in New York City. He and June were members of the New York Choral Society and are talented musicians (during one of my visits, they were both trying, with great difficulty, to memorize the challenging Latin words to *Carmina Burana* for upcoming performances). They have taken trips to Central America for many years to improve their Spanish by immersion. Both have been involved in social ministries and causes, working tirelessly on the front lines.

They are people who put their faith into action. And they love from the center of who they are in God. I have often said that Jim and June are my heroes—they represent the kind of person I want to be: active, energetic, giving, loving, authentic, and amazing.

When I read these verses from the letter to the Romans, I think of Jim and June and Colin—and so many other friends and loved ones God has brought into my life.

I think of good friends who love deeply, who live and love like Jesus, who beckon me to join them in living the radically loving life of God in the power of the Spirit.

Who are your heroes, your friends in the faith? How can you outdo them in love?

❧

Holy Spirit, being the kind of person you call me to be requires putting my little fears, my selfish habits, my self-centered ways, my false masks aside and being real, loving deeply from my center with the love you have lavished on me. This is what I want. This is what I choose. Let's go. Amen.

18. Getting Along

> Live in harmony with one another; do not be
> haughty, but associate with the lowly; do not
> claim to be wiser than you are. Do not repay
> anyone evil for evil but take thought for what is
> noble in the sight of all. If it is possible, so far
> as it depends on you, live peaceably with all.
> —ROMANS 12:16-18

I'm certainly not the most gregarious person in the world. But
I've learned time and again how much fun it is to step out,
reach out, and engage other people.

It's always such a nice surprise to speak to someone who
doesn't expect to be spoken to—a fellow passenger on the
elevator, a restaurant server, a landscaper, a grocery store
cashier, a homeless person, the churchgoer you've never met
sitting in the pew ahead of you.

Usually, we ignore people like that, and they ignore us. But
I'm always amazed at how their countenance—and mine, for
that matter—changes when I try to engage them. The frown
fades. Their face lights up. They chuckle. They enter into the
conversation. Suddenly, we seem to be old friends.

Not everyone is open to such engagement, of course. Unfortunately, some people won't accept this invitation from Romans. Just the other day, I tried and tried to engage a gentleman in conversation, asking questions, cracking a joke or two, and he simply wouldn't have it. He certainly seemed to have gotten up on the wrong side of the bed that morning. I'll admit, I've been that person sometimes too, and it's not a happy place to be.

If we would all start to take this Spirit-invitation seriously, we'd find our days brighter, thanks to these little light interludes of interaction. And who knows, those moments may open the door to something more.

Ordinarily when I'm on an airplane, I keep to myself. I'm usually tired, frazzled from the complicated process of getting to the airport, through security, and then on board. But I'm always so glad when I make an effort to be friendly with my seatmates.

On one late-evening flight from Baltimore back home to Atlanta, I sat next to a man who appeared to be somewhat frustrated and nervous. I don't remember who started the small talk, but it soon grew to an open and mutually encouraging conversation between two siblings in Christ that lasted until after we landed. I'm sure we distracted those around us trying to catch some shuteye.

Darren was heading through Atlanta for Florida to meet his young daughter and wife, who had flown down earlier to be with her family after her mother had fallen seriously ill. He had been delayed in order to take the test to become a Pennsylvania state trooper—a test he unfortunately had failed. He was not having a good day.

We talked together about how God uses such difficult times and frustrations. He encouraged me, I think, more than I did him. At any rate, our spirits were mutually lifted through the mystery of siblinghood.

Toward the end of our conversation, we both acknowledged that we rarely talked to our fellow passengers. But God had opened this door, and we had entered it gladly together. Darren and I remained sporadically in touch via email, sharing the latest news. Sometime later, I received an email from him with a link to a collection of photos from his recent family reunion.

A similar thing occurred on a flight to a preaching conference some years ago, when I discovered my young seatmate was heading there himself. He was preparing the sermon that he would present on the Beatitudes, and the wisdom he shared from his study of the opening verses blew my mind and blessed my soul—and has shown up in my own sermons on that text. He now pastors a large and vibrant church, and I am delighted to keep in touch with him through social media.

Experiences like these encourage me to keep reaching out to whoever I run into when the opportunity arises.

I want to be aware of others around me, not oblivious to them. I want to see the beauty, the nobility, in each person's soul. That is the way to peace, harmony, joy, and love.

⚜

Holy Spirit help me be in harmony with whomever I encounter today—even those I might usually not give a second glance. Help me to see the divine beauty within each person, to sense our common human bonds, to sense a holy connection through our relationship with you. Amen.

19. Friends with God

> We entreat you on behalf of Christ, be
> reconciled to God. For our sake he made him
> to be sin who knew no sin, so that in him we
> might become the righteousness of God.
> —2 CORINTHIANS 5:20B, 21

❧

How do we become "reconciled to God"?

"Become friends with God; he's already a friend with you.
How? you ask. In Christ. God put the wrong on him who
never did anything wrong, so we could be put right with God"
(2 Corinthians 5:20b, 21, *The Message*).

Think about the friends in your life. Recall how you met them,
how you "became friends." What were the circumstances? How
did you feel when you met them? Did you immediately click,
or did it take some time?

So many friends come to my mind. Some have come into and
gone out of my life. Others have been part of my circle of
support for many years. Still others I'm just getting to know.

I think of the friend I met on his first day on the job at the
organization we both worked for, a fellow writer and movie

buff who showed me how fun friendship can be. He moved away with his new bride for graduate school but wrote me long letters that I responded to enthusiastically. He has become an encourager to me in tough times just as I hope I have been for him in his tough times. We had lunch occasionally, even more than three decades after we met, until he and his wife (I married them) moved to Florida. But we keep in touch.

I think of the friend I met nearly twenty years ago through our *Day 1* website who had been searching online for "sermons" and found us. He lives in Germany, and he and I have shared our life's struggles and joys by email and messaging and photos, even to this day.

I think of the guy I'd seen at my church but didn't really meet until we were on a retreat, where we bonded as brothers in a deep and spiritual way.

I think of the dozen friends I have gotten to know over the past three decades through an email discussion group—half of whom I've met in "real life," all pretty much old guys like me who grew up reading comic books and who now live across America, in England and Australia.

I think of the many amazing friends I have gotten to know through my spouse, with whom we often enjoy wonderful dinners and take museum tours and travel and do other fun activities together.

I think of my best friend, my husband, Dan. When I met him more than fifteen years ago, I knew he was the one for me. He has helped me stretch and grow with encouragement and wisdom and creativity. On and on and on, the friends go through my mind.

Who are your friends? How did you get to know them? What are the common denominators? For me, these connectors are:

✤ An immediate acceptance of each other

✤ A chemistry of mutual interests

✤ A lively desire to get to know each other better

✤ A yearning to do things together—fun or work or ministry or just life

✤ A willingness to share and work through the difficult times together

✤ An eagerness to help each other out

✤ A spark of contact and bonding that simply cannot be defined

✤ An amazing weaving together of the hearts through open, honest communication with each other, often as a result of standing together through very difficult times

Now, do you sense these common denominators with God? They are there if you look. Through Christ, God already possesses them toward you—God is already your friend. You are reconciled to God as a beloved child.

Somehow it seems trifling to think of your relationship with God as a friendship. God is so much more—the Creator and Redeemer and Sustainer of the universe. Being a friend of this God seems to trivialize who God really is. Doesn't it?

Don't let it. God wants you to draw closer. God wants to be your friend.

The Bible is full of examples of people who became God's friends. Moses was called a friend of God, for God spoke with Moses face to face (Exodus 33:11). David was called "a man after God's own heart" (Acts 13:22). In 2 Corinthians 5:20-21, the apostle Paul declares that the Lord already considers himself your friend.

Human friendships are among the most powerful forces in the universe. Think how much more powerful your friendship with God could be.

Accept the invitation to experience the lifelong love, fulfillment, and purpose of being God's close friend.

Holy Spirit, thank you for the friends you have brought into my world, those who have enriched my life in the past and those who continue to do so now and in the future. Help me keep my primary relationship with God, my closest friend, growing and vibrant and mutually enjoyable. Help me to get to know you better so that my heart may beat as yours. And help me to share you with others. Amen.

20. Living Deeply

> And now, little children, abide in him, so that
> when he is revealed we may have confidence
> and not be put to shame before him at his
> coming. —1 JOHN 2:28

◦⊗◦

Abide in Christ.

I love the word abide, but it's not used very often these days.

Recently the subject of abiding came up in a discussion I had
with one of our *Day 1* preachers. After the recording session,
we got to talking about the Gospel of John—the source of
the passage she had preached on. She told me that one of the
things about John's Gospel she appreciates is the emphasis on
abiding—an emphasis carried through in this epistle that also
bears his name.

But what does it mean to "abide in Christ"? *The Message*
captures the sense well: "stay with Christ... live deeply in
Christ." It means making yourself at home continually in
Jesus's loving presence.

Saint Teresa of Avila knew about abiding. Born in Spain in
1515, Teresa became a nun in the Carmelite convent—even

though she was considered a spoiled and unimpressive young woman. Over the years, her fervent faith emerged as she instituted reforms in her order. Known for her ecstasies in the presence of God, Teresa wrote several beloved classics of spiritual literature.

Every night Teresa would converse with Jesus. One evening Jesus asked Teresa her name. Teresa replied, "Teresa of Jesus." She then turned the table and asked Jesus his name. She heard him respond, "Jesus of Teresa."[6]

Think about that.

Most of us yearn for a relationship with God like this. A relationship that is deep, personal, meaningful, solid, trustworthy, real. A relationship that is unusual in a culture marked by shallow roots and superficiality.

How do we build an abiding relationship with Jesus?

We build it the same way we develop a relationship with our best friend or spouse. We spend time talking. And listening. Spending time together. Helping others together. Going deep with each other. Sharing the day's events and viewpoints with each other. Laughing and crying together. Trusting each other. Being as honest and open with each other as possible. Being ourselves—no masks, no pretenses, no faking.

So that's what we do with Jesus.

Do it, and keep doing it, and soon we will be living deeply. We will be abiding.

And when we are abiding, we are ready to receive God with open arms. Honestly, freely, without shame or embarrassment.

⊷❧⊶

Holy Spirit, draw me closer to Jesus, every moment, every day. I want to be real with you, deep with you, open with you, so I can be ready for all those times you want to do something spectacular in and through me. Amen.

The Spirit Beckons You to Community

21. Creative Care

> Contribute to the needs of the saints; extend hospitality to strangers. —ROMANS 12:13

The Spirit beckons you now into a way of life that exemplifies inventive, generous hospitality, meeting the needs of fellow members of the family of faith in creative ways.

How many times have you and I been the beneficiary of that sort of generous hospitality? Life is full of the blessings of such hospitality.

When I was in seminary in Dallas with my young family many years ago, I was required to do a thirteen-week internship in a local church. The huge church I attended was crawling with seminarians, so it was tough to find an internship position there that would provide a full taste of local church ministry.

I really wanted that exposure, a complete exposure to pastoral life. As the son of a minister, I wrestled with the particularities of my call. I sensed God was calling me to seminary not to prepare for a pastoral ministry but to equip me to serve in a communications capacity, especially writing about faith. But I wanted to test that and be open to the Spirit's leading.

I could have chosen to teach a junior high Sunday school class at any one of a number of Dallas mega-churches and check off this obligation. But I wanted to become immersed in a local church and see for myself if my gifts, such as they were, fit the requirements of the job.

As I continued my search, one day I noticed a three-by-five card on a seminary bulletin board covered with ministry opportunities. The Church of the Master, a small United Church of Christ congregation in South Dallas, sought a student assistant. I called the pastor, Jerry, who eagerly urged me to come visit. Apparently, that notecard had been posted on that bulletin board for many months without a single response.

I ended up serving as the unpaid student assistant pastor at the Church of the Master for about a year. They met in a shopping center storefront, about fifty folks on a Sunday morning, most of them middle-age and older Whites in a swiftly, ethnically changing community. With a dwindling membership, they had been forced to sell their nearby church building a year or so earlier.

They were a precious flock, and they put up with my inexperience. Jerry had me preach to them once a month, teach a youth Sunday school class weekly, and help lead a Wednesday night Bible study. I attended just about every church meeting, joined with volunteers to get the newsletters ready to mail, and visited sick members in the hospital with Jerry. I even observed while Jerry offered premarital counseling to an engaged couple.

I did everything you could possibly do in a small local church. On top of a regular load of classes and a couple of part-time paying jobs, it stretched me to the max, but it taught me volumes about hospitality and love.

While the entire church welcomed my little family and me, one family held us especially close to their hearts. Jessie was a widow with a heart as big as her neatly kept home. Her daughters, Millie and Martha, both in their fifties, had inherited the generosity gene from their mother. They made our little orphan family, far away from our home in West Virginia, part of their family.

Every holiday—Easter, Thanksgiving, July 4, whatever—they invited us to join their extended family for an incredible meal and loving family fellowship. When my son Matthew was born during that year, they were as giddy as grandmothers, all three of them.

We were welcomed. Loved. And made part of the family.

Toward the end of that internship year, Millie's health failed. I got the call that she had been rushed to intensive care at a nearby hospital. Part of my job as the pastoral assistant was to help Jerry minister to the family. We prayed and held hands and waited. I still remember seeing Millie in a coma, her little round body at the mercy of a ventilator, causing her lungs to inhale and exhale at a surprising and noisy pace, and feeling so helpless.

Millie passed away quickly. Jessie and Martha were devastated by the unexpected loss—Millie was the youngest, after all. One of the most difficult tasks I ever had to do there was to help Jerry with the funeral service. How do you manage to minister to the grieving when you're one of them? I had to learn the hard way.

That internship year ended, and it was time for me to prepare for the next phase of my life after graduation. But we had become part of the family. And always would be.

Jessie died not long after we moved to Atlanta. But we kept in touch for some years with Martha. Nowadays, the Church of the Master has been lost to history. The membership continued to dwindle, and they eventually closed the storefront sanctuary. But that little church family will live forever, in my heart and I'm sure in many others' hearts, because they were inventive and generous in hospitality.

It's not that difficult to fulfill this holy imperative. Yes, it might be inconvenient and feel a little scary at times to reach out. But the joy and love that result from helping other needy believers, building community with them, and welcoming them into your heart, lasts forever.

❧

Holy Spirit, you have ministered to me through so many dear, creatively loving people. Help me to share their love and inventive care with those who desperately need it in the family of God so that together we can reach out to a world that so rarely experiences love and acceptance. Surprise me with such an opportunity today. And let me be ready for it. Amen.

22. Laughter and Tears

Rejoice with those who rejoice, weep with those
who weep. —ROMANS 12:15

⬥

When my friend wept uncontrollably as he told me about his
broken engagement, my heart felt like it was broken in nearly
as many places as his was.

Yet months later, as he enjoyed a renewed and deepened
relationship with the same woman, we found ourselves
laughing to tears at the turn of events and about the
unexpected surprises God so often brings into our lives.

This is what it means to be members of the body of Christ,
the family of God: sharing the joyful times, the happy times,
the times of success and achievement and breakthrough and
glory. And: sharing the sorrowful times, the painful, pleading,
disappointed times, the times of loss and grief and shame.

Something amazing and powerful happens when we share with
others at this level. Together, in community, our joy increases
and our sadness lessens. We strengthen each other, teach each
other, learn from one another, and bond with each other.
With one another and God those bonds can be unbreakable.

We become exponentially more powerful and fruitful together than we are alone.

Sometimes, honestly, we would rather not bother. We have enough troubles and issues of our own. It takes time and effort and energy to get involved so closely in others' lives that they matter to us. Suffering and weeping with others in pain and misery is not easy. It hurts. It drains.

But it's worth it. And even if it wasn't worth it, it's what the Spirit invites us into: the mysterious eternal fellowship of the beloved.

It takes effort to become close to others—authentically bonded together. It's an intentional act to care, to support, to listen, to share. And while the light times of laughter and joy may be bright and enjoyable, the shadow times are part of the whole deal.

The wondrous thing in sharing so closely with others in community, whether they are celebrating or mourning, is that those others will be with you in your times of celebrating and mourning. This is what it means to be family.

❦

Holy Spirit, I offer my thanks for the family of faith you have surrounded me with, to encourage and prod me, mourn and laugh with me, listen to me, love me. Help me to do the same with them, to be the friend and sibling they need in the dark times and the bright times. Amen.

23. *A Humble Welcome*

Welcome those who are weak in faith, but not
for the purpose of quarreling over opinions.
—Romans 14:1

❧

Churches—and whole denominations—can be hotbeds of
controversy. And in times of troubling differences involving
fundamental issues of faith, theology, and cultural norms,
there's no telling how people who disagree with each other will
treat each other.

In 2003, I attended the Episcopal General Convention in
Minneapolis where Gene Robinson's election as Bishop of New
Hampshire was ratified. The convention center was marked by
tension and anger inside and out. Gene, the first openly gay
man elected as bishop, was advised to wear a bullet-proof vest
for fear of the rowdy homophobic crowds gathered outside
hurling vicious taunts, venting their spleens.

Two weeks later, in the very same convention center, I
attended another denomination's general synod. This
convention was marked by joy, with rainbow flags abounding;
a transgender choir sang. A lesbian church leader raised
the rafters with her preaching. This denomination had

already dealt with the fundamental issue of allowing—even encouraging—anyone to be part of their church no matter how God had created them.

In the years since, most of the mainline denominations have dealt—usually painfully—with the LGBTQIA+ issue, as well as many others. Nevertheless, some still struggle and face rancorous splits in the face of disagreements.

Is this what the Spirit invites us to? Consider prayerfully this verse from Romans. What does it tell us about "quarreling over opinions"?

Once again, Eugene Peterson fleshes out the invitation:

> Welcome with open arms fellow believers who don't see things the way you do. And don't jump all over them every time they do or say something you don't agree with—even when it seems that they are strong on opinions but weak in the faith department. Remember, they have their own history to deal with. Treat them gently (Romans 14:1, *The Message*).

God's invitation is simple:

✚ Welcome others authentically and wholly.

✚ Don't jump down their throats when they say something you don't agree with.

✚ Realize that they've come to their views as a result of their own history—just as you have.

✚ Treat them gently.

Perhaps your disagreement is not theological—it might be a decision someone has made that you think is unwise. By all means, share your thoughts with that person, but do it gently and lovingly.

This is not an easy assignment. When we feel that what we believe is right, it's difficult to accept the right of others to disagree.

God's Spirit beckons us to converse with others with whom we disagree, to commune with them, to interact with mutual respect and tolerance and grace, while embracing fellowship with gentleness and sensitivity.

Out of that kind of relationship in community, new things can happen. God can work. The Spirit can change hearts and minds. And we can honor and serve Jesus together.

Is it possible? Yes. I've seen it happen many times. The Spirit who invites us into this sort of dialogue is able to give the strength and guidance to make it so.

But it begins with an intentional decision to be in community.

Holy Spirit, sometimes I wish you would just tell all of us the right answers to life's toughest questions, the most controversial issues. But you choose to build wisdom and maturity in us by forcing us to get along and find our way together in your power. Help us along the way to respect one another, to welcome one another, admire your work in each other's lives, and treat one another with gentleness. Open our minds and hearts to the way you work in that process. Amen.

24. Consider the Source

> Consider your own call, brothers and sisters:
> not many of you were wise by human
> standards, not many were powerful, not many
> were of noble birth. —1 CORINTHIANS 1:26

The Spirit takes us down a notch—keeps us real: "Consider your own call"—take a good look at yourself and remember who you are—because not many of you are wise, or powerful, or of noble birth.

Disagreement and division rocked the church community at Corinth. The apostle sought to bring the various sides back to reality so they could realize their need for one another, their mutual dependency on Christ, their equality before the cross.

Take a good look. Look beyond your posturing and your public façade and see reality: God accepts anyone into the community of faith, no matter what their background, their personality, their quirks, their predispositions, their race, their social status, their gender identity, their orientation, or their financial status might be.

Take a good look. And realize this: "God chose what is *foolish* in the world to shame the wise; God chose what is *weak* in the world to shame the strong; God chose what is *low* and *despised* in the world, things that are not, to reduce to nothing things that are, so that no one might boast in the presence of God" (1 Corithians 1:27-29, emphasis added).

Take a good look. And acknowledge that you don't bring anything any more extraordinary to the table than anyone else does. Everyone is gifted and blessed by God to take part in the common cause of Christ. And we desperately need each other.

Take a good look. And marvel that we really don't create or accomplish anything, but that everything we have, everything we are, comes from God through Jesus Christ. "[God] is the source of your life in Christ Jesus, who became for us wisdom from God, and righteousness and sanctification and redemption, in order that, as it is written, 'Let the one who boasts, boast in the Lord'" (1 Corinthians 1:30-31).

Take a good look. What do you see?

Holy Spirit, I am thankful for the redemption of my soul and my life. Help me keep this miracle of God in perspective—that it's not the result of anything I've done, and that it doesn't make me any better than anyone else. Help me take a good look at my attitudes toward others and to baptize those attitudes in the love and grace of your will. Amen.

25. What Loving People Do

Greet all the brothers and sisters with a holy
kiss. —1 Thessalonians 5:26

⌘

Bible translators have had a difficult time making this
verse work in our culture and time. It can make us feel
uncomfortable.

Eugene Peterson tried to contemporize the expression by
replacing "holy kiss" with "holy embrace." In other words, give
each other a holy hug. But even the idea of hugging those we
don't know well can make many of us squirm. And pandemics
only make things worse.

But I suppose "holy embrace" is preferable to the wording in
J. B. Philips's translation of this verse: "Give a handshake all
round among the brotherhood." Though I wince even more at
his attempt at the same verbiage in Romans 16:16: "A hearty
handshake all around!" Very British.

Even the note on this verse in the *NIV Study Bible* coyly
explains, "A kiss was a normal greeting of that day, similar to
our modern handshake."

Why are we afraid of this verse? Yes, our culture is different. But maybe we should recapture that passionate affection for one another in the community of Christ.

This thought occurred to me when I read an article on Christian counselor and author Larry Crabb in *Christianity Today*. A passage about the "spontaneously begun ritual" Crabb and his spiritual mentor, the late Brennan Manning, followed whenever they saw each other, jumped out at me:

> "As soon as we spot one another," says Manning, "we both jump up and down, run to one another, and kiss one another on the lips."
>
> "Why do you do that?" I ask Manning.
>
> "It's the sheer delight in seeing one another," he says. "When you see two men in public doing that, there's often only one conclusion. But he's so secure in his identity that we can throw caution to the wind. If anybody's got a problem with that, then it's their problem."[7]

Other than dealing with pandemics, what has happened to our culture that has made outward signs of affection so unacceptable? Oh, I occasionally do the air kisses next to someone's cheek—a dear sister or female friend. But I don't think that's what the writer had in mind here.

Yes, there is the risk of going too far, of acting in ways that aren't appropriate or invited. I suppose that's why translators and scholars try to help us feel more comfortable with this verse. But maybe we've lost far more than we've gained.

I want to live in the tension of this divine invitation. I want to feel the camaraderie and mutual love with my siblings in my fellowships of faith to the extent that the Spirit encourages it here.

Sure, it was probably just a throwaway line the apostle wrote as he wrapped up his letter to the believers in Thessalonica. They likely didn't give it a second thought, as it was a cultural norm for them to express affection this way. Look at current Latin American, European, Asian, or Middle Eastern social practices and you'll find they tend to be much more affectionate with each other—fathers and sons, brothers, friends.

Maybe in our culture we've lost something precious.

Here's what I want to wrestle with: how might I express my sheer delight in my siblings in the community of faith when I see them—in ways that are acceptable and safe and yet still passionate and free?

❧

Holy Spirit, thank you for the precious, beloved siblings in the faith you've put in my life. Help me show them in righteous ways how much I love and appreciate them. Let them know how deeply loved they are—by me and by you. Amen.

The Spirit Beckons You to Harmony

26. Living in Peace

> Put things in order, listen to my appeal,
> agree with one another, live in peace; and
> the God of love and peace will be with you.
> —2 CORINTHIANS 13:11B

The apostle, as usual, makes it sound so easy: just do these few things, and everything will be great, full of love and peace.

It sure sounds appealing. It's definitely what I want to experience. How realistic is it in this world?

Thanks be to God, *through Jesus Christ...* I guess.

I experienced the exact opposite of all these things over the course of several months one time. The deck on my home back then was getting very wobbly, certainly not in good order. It was nearly twenty-five years old; the wood was gray and wrinkled and splinter inducing. And it shook when you walked on it. That's not a good feeling when you're 16 feet off the ground.

People replace decks all the time without much hassle. And several deck-experienced friends offered to help. We could easily take down the old one and put up the new one in one weekend. Simple, right? Wrong.

I decided to do things right and go to the county for a permit. I had to have a map of our lot and show where the deck would be, along with a $50 check and a good deal of patience. Several people asked me, "Why did you bother getting a permit? It's no big deal." But I thought it was the right thing to do. Plus, some neighbors up the street were putting a big addition on their home, and county inspectors would be in the neighborhood. I didn't want them to smell the burning sawdust and find my outlaw deck under construction. Can you go to jail for replacing a deck without a permit? I didn't want to find out.

Of course, even with all the help I had, the process was far more difficult, complicated, and exhausting than expected. It took several weeks to get a list of lumber and supplies we'd need, as I consulted with two different home improvement stores to make sure we would have everything necessary. It wouldn't be cheap, but at least the labor was free—except for the pizzas and beer we had to buy.

The weekend we did the work went rather well. We worked in harmony and camaraderie. With several guys (other than me) who were experienced do-it-yourselfers and deck-builders, we managed to tear down the old deck and set up the new, improved version rather efficiently. It took three days (over a Labor Day weekend), but we got the deck and the steps and railings and everything put together handsomely. But my, were those big pieces of lumber heavy.

The next week, I called the county inspector to come check out our handiwork. When I got home later that day, I found a big red "warning" tag attached to the permit sign out in front of my home.

We'd flunked. The county was prohibiting us from using the deck until several things were fixed, to wit: the railings on the stairs were one inch—*one measly inch*—below the required height. The stair railings were also improperly fashioned—the way we had done it, the warning said, created a virtual ladder for little children who could plunge to great injury over the railings. Also, we had attached the whole deck incorrectly to the house—lag *bolts*, not *screws*, were required now. And we forgot to insert flashing—thin sheets of aluminum—between the deck and home to prevent water running behind the deck and rotting it away from the house. And, oh yes, we missed several nails on the joist holders. And on and on and on.

What little cheerfulness, agreeableness, harmony, and high spirits I had left were quickly dashed.

I called the inspector, trying not to lash out in frustrated anger, and asked him, "How were we supposed to know the specifics of the county code, so that we could have built it right in the first place?" After all, there had been no information provided at the county permit office. It wasn't available online. And neither of the home improvement stores would provide any guidance at all.

"You're just supposed to know it," the inspector said, as though that made perfect sense. "Or else ask us specific questions." I couldn't tell him that if I'd *known* what specific questions to ask, I *would* have asked him. He added that he understood that the home improvement stores had a policy *not* to tell customers the code rules, because if they didn't get it exactly right their DIY customers might be litigiously furious with the wrong advice. So, they don't say anything—not even a hint.

Of course, my big construction team was long gone now. It took one friend and me, with occasional help from others, the next four full weekends to make things right. We had to completely tear down the new stair railings we'd built and start over. It took us a long time to figure out how to get the flashing in between the house and the deck that had already been attached to it. Somehow, we managed it.

Then the re-inspection. This time, thankfully, only some minor finishing up was required. Eventually, our deck was declared officially safe. And we could have a legal cookout on it.

Some months later, most of the folks who'd helped us build the new deck celebrated the accomplishment right on that deck. We cheerfully recounted the horrifying tale, realizing that our house would fall down before this deck did.

I think of that incredibly complicated and stressful process and wonder what would have happened if I had maintained a cheerful attitude while keeping things "in order." What if I had kept my spirits up instead of becoming so exasperated and angry and frustrated and overwhelmed? What if I had strived to think in harmony instead of focusing on everyone's shortcomings and our inspector's demanding ways? What if I had simply tried to be agreeable?

When I really want to learn something about myself, I step back from that experience and realize that too often I approach my life, my work, my relationships with the same negative attitudes, the same exasperation and frustration, out of harmony with God's will for me. It feels like my whole life is about complicated deck building and inspector-satisfying.

Then I read these words written long ago to the Corinthians believers, and I let them wash over me. And inspire me. And fill me with spiritual focus:

"Be cheerful. Keep things in good repair. Keep your spirits up. Think in harmony. Be agreeable. Do all that, and the God of love and peace will be with you for sure" (2 Corinthians 13:11-14, *The Message*).

❦

Holy Spirit, these simple words communicate a generous invitation to a life of love and peace—the kind of life I yearn to experience. By your power, make these words real in my life. Help me keep my focus on living harmoniously and purposefully in your Spirit. So that whatever happens, you guide my response. Amen.

27. Just Like God

> Put away from you all bitterness and wrath
> and anger and wrangling and slander, together
> with all malice, and be kind to one another,
> tenderhearted, forgiving one another, as God in
> Christ has forgiven you. —EPHESIANS 4:31-32

&c.

If only we would do this.

Wouldn't it transform the national political discourse?
Wouldn't it transform our marriages? Wouldn't it bring
harmony to our relationships with our children? With our co-
workers and neighbors? With our church leaders?

The apostle makes it seem so easy—as we've seen he is wont
to do. Maybe it *is* easy, if we just "put away" all that negative
stuff. To simply determine in the power of the Spirit to stop
the bitter talk. To decide proactively to be gentle with others,
sensitive to their needs and situation, tenderhearted toward
those in need. To be eager to forgive and hungry for harmony.

Do you want that in your life? I do. I want to put it all away.

As I write this, I am grieved by the situation in a marriage of
a couple I know well. They are good people. They are loving,

responsible, and generally positive. For several reasons, they are treating each other viciously. Their life is miserable, and they are considering ending the relationship.

Yes, there are issues galore: longstanding problems stemming from all sorts of bad influences, childhood memories, immature choices, and so forth. Those issues could be dealt with in maturity and love if they would simply choose to be kind and tenderhearted with each other, if they would forgive each other as God forgave them. But they have both been wounded so deeply by each other—through cutting, backbiting, profane talk and actions toward one another.

Can they make a clean break from all that negativity? I honestly don't know. It's so easy to give up when the situation reaches this point, to run away, believing the relationship is irredeemable. I pray that somehow God will blast through their pain and hurt and negativity with the fresh wind of healing and forgiveness and understanding and love. But will they let God do that?

You know people in similar situations. Maybe you are one of them.

What would it look like if you took this scripture seriously?

How hard would it be to change the tone of your voice? To begin building up your partner rather than tearing them down? To seek harmony rather than fight to be right?

The Spirit invites us to "put away" all our past negative, destructive behavior. That really can happen only with the power of the Spirit. And it may seem totally one-sided at first as you pursue this new way of living. But I have seen redemption and healing in such broken relationships too many times to doubt that it can happen. If one wants it to happen.

If you are struggling in the negative, downward spiral of backbiting and hurtful talk, God beckons to you to put it away. Trust God and make the choice to go for reconciliation, healing, and harmony.

Then watch how the Spirit can, in time, provide the balm of love and forgiveness.

❧

Holy Spirit, I confess I open my mouth far too quickly and say things much too negatively. How this can help any situation, I don't know. All I know is that it's my natural reaction to pain and fear. But you are supernatural. And your Spirit is with me, ready to empower me to put away this behavior—at least to start making steps in that direction. Thank you for forgiving me so completely and readily. Help me share that forgiveness in authentic and powerful ways. Amen.

28. Keep On Keeping On

> Keep on doing the things that you have learned
> and received and heard and seen in me, and the
> God of peace will be with you.
> —PHILIPPIANS 4:9

⊗

Years ago, my son Matt and I enjoyed going camping occasionally, usually to Fort Yargo or Hard Labor Creek state parks in Georgia. One summer when Matt was about to leave for college, we decided it would be good to get one more camping trip in before he left the family nest.

This time, Matt didn't want to camp at one of those wimpy state parks with water faucets and restrooms and flat pads to pitch a tent on. He wanted a more primitive site. I thought of a favorite site in North Georgia where we had camped years earlier. It was a gorgeously wooded area just off the Richard Russell Scenic Highway.

As I recalled, you had to really know where you were going in order to find it because the Forest Service road wasn't marked. But once you found your way there, you'd have your choice of three or four nice campsites along the roaring creek. A nearby meadow offered a great vantage point to gaze at the stars. Across the creek and down a way was a switchback trail that led to the spectacular Duke's Creek Falls.

So that's where we'd head this time. We drove up around noon that Saturday and, armed with internet maps, found the location again with no problem.

But things had changed.

The Duke's Creek area had become part of the Raven Cliffs Wilderness Area and Smithgall Woods. The spot where we had camped a few years earlier was now in the process of being changed, upgraded, with a new gravel parking lot, improved roads, and—I could hardly believe it—restroom facilities.

Not only that, it had a new name. A fresh Forest Service sign—still partially covered with plastic because it wasn't officially ready yet—announced the site as "Raven Cliffs Trail Head."

It hardly looked like a primitive area anymore. I couldn't get my bearings—it was clearly the same place I remembered, but it looked and felt so different. Construction debris was piled everywhere. It was messy and confusing. I didn't like the changes.

But we pitched our tent on a large and lovely campsite right beside the rushing creek. Only one other couple had chosen to camp in the area, and they were a good distance away from us.

Nobody else showed up—probably because we had torrential thunderstorms that weekend. We enjoyed ourselves despite the rain.

Well, isn't that just like life? No matter how much we want things to remain the same, they change. We experience changes in our job, relationships, and circumstances. Inevitably change causes us to lose our bearings and feel uncomfortable. All of us experienced this phenomenon during the COVID-19 pandemic.

But if we live determined to accept God's generous beckoning to come closer, then we can be assured that, ultimately, the change will be for the better. The process may be confusing and messy and even painful. It can make us ache for the old ways of life and question God's good sense, but, "God, who makes everything work together, will work you into his most excellent harmonies" (*The Message*, Philippians 4:9).

Someday, we can look back at all the earth-shattering changes we experience in life and realize what happened to us and through us as a result of them. And we will see that it was good. That it was all part of God's "most excellent harmonies."

That's why I have a feeling that, one day, I'll head back to my favorite campsite by Duke's Creek and be able to enjoy the beauty of creation there—as well as the new restroom facilities.

Holy Spirit, thank you for the promise of obedient, authentic faith. I yearn to be part of God's most excellent harmonies, everything working together—even the drastic, confusing changes in life—for the glory of God. Amen.

29. The Indwelling Word

> Let the word of Christ dwell in you richly;
> teach and admonish one another in all
> wisdom; and with gratitude in your hearts sing
> psalms, hymns, and spiritual songs to God.
> And whatever you do, in word or deed, do
> everything in the name of the Lord Jesus,
> giving thanks to God the Father through
> him. —COLOSSIANS 3:16-17

⚜

I wonder what our lives would look like if we let the word of Christ fully dwell within us—or to "Let the Word of Christ... have the run of the house" (Colossians 3:16, *The Message*). Imagine that!

What might happen if we let the way of love run amok in our hearts? If we gave the Spirit of God plenty of room in our souls, opening ourselves to allow the Spirit to run loose within us, with no hesitation, no holding back, no fear about what might happen if we lost control? Strange things could happen indeed.

We might discover a mutual support system with our siblings in the faith, "teaching and admonishing," instructing and cautioning each other in the spirit of love and truth and mercy.

We might uncork a stream of common sense for living, so we start making choices with God's big picture in mind instead of reacting out of fear or selfishness.

We might find our hearts lifted in gratitude, singing and soaring in praise as a matter of routine.

We might live out every detail of our lives wholly conscious of Jesus's invitations to us, seeking to follow him more intentionally in the way of love, wherever he might lead.

We might take every step, every day, every moment, with a heart full of thanks for the heavenly God who provides our every need and promises an eternity filled with everlasting love and praise.

We might actually live in harmony with God and with one another.

Do you sense the gracious invitation to let the word of Christ dwell within you—starting right now?

Isn't that an invitation worth accepting?

❧

Holy Spirit, your word is life. Fill my heart and soul with it, let it fill me to overflowing. Let it run amok in my heart. Let me walk in obedience and love with eternal thanks. Amen.

The Spirit Beckons You to Joy

30. Drink Up

Do not get drunk with wine, for that is debauchery; but be filled with the Spirit, as you sing psalms and hymns and spiritual songs among yourselves, singing and making melody to the Lord in your hearts, giving thanks to God the Father at all times and for everything in the name of our Lord Jesus Christ.
—Ephesians 5:18-20

When I began attending an Episcopal church in the early 1990s, after years in conservative evangelical churches, I wondered if I would find taking communion every week to be a bit much.

I mean, with eucharist at just about every church service, even several times through the week, wouldn't it begin to lose its meaning, its impact? Wouldn't it become so rote and emptily ritualistic as to lose all sense of importance? Wouldn't it become boring?

What I've discovered is that nothing could be further from the truth. In fact, when the time comes, I can't wait to approach the communion rail.

The coronavirus pandemic only made my love for the eucharist even more deep because we were not allowed to partake, save perhaps through spiritual communion or communion in one kind for months on end.

In the Episcopal tradition, we use wine in our communion service. White-robed chalice bearers offer a cup, and we intinct the bread in the wine or sip gently from the cup, recalling the death of Christ on our behalf. It may be the old, old story, but it never really gets old.

I think of that communion cup as I read this passage. The context is different—the apostle isn't speaking of the eucharist, although in some cases he had trouble with churches who let their *agape* meals get way out of hand, becoming a drunken party. But I admit that sometimes I am so hungry for God's presence that I feel like grabbing that chalice and chugging it down.

Wine can lift the spirit, but it's an artificial, temporary lift. Alcohol is a depressant, weighing down the heart. There is another way to lift the spirit—one that has an immensely greater impact on our lives:

"Be filled with the Spirit." Or, "Drink the Spirit of God, huge draughts…" (Ephesians 5:18, *The Message*). Fill up with the Holy Spirit of God. Guzzle the Spirit down.

How do we do that? It starts with being open in heart, mind, and spirit. Intentionally seeking God's presence through prayer and meditation. Yearning for God's cool, clean, rejuvenating spiritual refreshment.

Sometimes singing hymns and praise songs can be both a cause and an effect of this joyful filling of the Spirit.

I don't know how many times I've been driving in achingly slow traffic in the early morning rush, weighed down by all sorts of concerns, grumbling in disappointment and discouragement, only to—by an act of sheer faith—call up on my phone a gorgeous anthem or praise song and find myself singing songs of worship and adoration at the top of my lungs.

My spirit is lifted. It soars. It is filled with joy. And by the time I arrive at my destination, I'm disappointed to have to leave my mobile sanctuary. But I take this spirit of singing with me throughout the day.

The Spirit beckons us to fill ourselves to overflowing with God's joy. It's not a one-time event; it's an ongoing, intentional action. No matter where we are, no matter what we're doing, sing and make "melody to the Lord in your hearts, giving thanks to God the Father at all times and for everything in the name of our Lord Jesus Christ."

Drink up. And sing heartily.

⸎

Holy Spirit, I yearn to be filled with your presence, your power, your purpose, your joy. Always. Let me hear the music of eternity in my soul, and empower me to sing along with everything I've got. Amen.

31. Godly Revelry

Rejoice in the Lord always; again I will say,
Rejoice. —Philippians 4:4

❧

If only I could put all this work aside...

If only I could reconcile with my wandering child...

If only I could get some control over my financial life ...

If only I could get my spouse to go to church with me...

If only my ailing parent would recuperate...

If only my boss would understand the stress I'm under...

If only my car would stop breaking down...

If only I didn't have to worry about getting sick...

If only...

If only life would cooperate, it would be easy to "celebrate
God all day, every day. I mean *revel* in him!" (Philippians 4:4,
The Message)

What was Paul thinking? He certainly couldn't understand the
pressures and pains that fill my life.

Oh, by the way, Paul was in prison when he wrote this verse to the Christians at Philippi. Paul was in shackles in a dark, squalid cell, chained to the wall, when he urged his fellow believers to revel joyfully in God.

So perhaps one's circumstances don't have to inhibit one's celebration.

But that makes no sense, my mind protests. *How could it possibly work?*

Beloved, what if we tried? What if, just for a few moments, we set aside our worries, fears, concerns, pains, hardships, circumstances, and *rejoiced* in God?

What might happen if we just let ourselves:

Praise God for the love and mercy lavished upon us…

Glorify God for the hope we can rely on through Christ…

Thank God for all the ways our needs are met sometimes unexpectedly…

Adore God for our many answered prayers.

Sing to the Lord and revel in God's presence. Just for a few minutes, right now. Then tomorrow, perhaps for a few minutes more. And for an hour or two early next week. Again, I will say, rejoice!

Before we know it, we'll be celebrating God all day, every day. No matter where we are, or what we're doing, or who we're with.

We have been invited to a party that never ends. RSVP.

Holy Spirit, thank you for your gracious invitation to celebrate God in my life. I hereby accept. And I plan to bring a guest or two. Amen.

32. Rejoicing Always

> Rejoice always, pray without ceasing, give
> thanks in all circumstances; for this is the
> will of God in Christ Jesus for you.
> —1 THESSALONIANS 5:16-18

❧

I had to go to the post office the other morning to pick up
a certified letter. The line was awfully long, and I had to
wait forever while the postal worker searched for my letter.
Meanwhile, an employee at the counter was greeting every
other person in line with the most outrageously friendly,
incessantly upbeat patter I think I have ever heard. The longer
I waited, the more irritated I became.

Frankly, people who are cheerful all the time annoy me.
They can't possibly be genuinely happy, can they? I'm usually
an upbeat, optimistic sort myself but not all the time. Let's
be real.

So why is the Spirit inviting us to a lifestyle that rejoices
always? Isn't this encouraging us to be inauthentic? Fakey? This
is the way God wants us to live?

Apparently. But perhaps the cheerfulness stems from the other
two imperatives: "pray without ceasing" and "give thanks in
all circumstances."

Maybe if we kept our hearts and spirits tuned to those pursuits, joy would follow.

As I think over my own history about the few people who seemed to authentically exemplify this three-fold invitation to obedience, Danita comes to my mind. She was a young woman, probably in her early twenties, with a head exploding with blonde curls. She loosely wore the gray uniform favored by our press operators at *The West Virginia Hillbilly* newspaper where I worked at the time.

Danita was one of the assistants who helped run the offset press. She was usually covered with ink, her clothes stained, her hands blackened, her face smudged. But she always had a positive word for everyone, a cheerful smile, no matter what seemed to be happening. When the press would break down or problems arose with the newspaper bailer, she'd simply go about the task of helping make things right, whistling exuberantly while she worked as though she were enjoying the challenge. She had a tender heart toward God. And it showed.

One of my dear aunts comes to mind, too. She has suffered far more than her fair share of heartbreak in life, losing a husband and a son. Yet her face always seems to glow with a genuine smile, a *shekinah* glory, a heart full of love and joy.

Bevel Jones, a beloved United Methodist bishop who became a mentor of mine, also comes to mind. He had such a rich and full life of ministry and remained deeply involved in the church and the community as long as he could. His good humor and cheerful wisdom couldn't help but rub off on everyone he met. His faith was unshakable because he had seen it tested time after time.

And Mrs. Melton rises in my memory. Every week she sat in the third-row pew with my sister Ann and me during our grade school days, while Dad conducted the Sunday morning service and Mom sang in the choir. Every week she'd bring pads of paper, pens, and various flavors of LifeSavers candies to keep us occupied and quiet during the service. Her constant smile and joyful good nature made her easy to obey and sit still.

Oh, there are many more I can think of. And I'm sure they all have their bad days. Yet they're all saints with whom I have enjoyed spending time. They have helped bring me back to God's reality and encouraged me to live fully in the joy of the Lord. No matter what.

Do I dare try to do the same for others?

❦

Holy Spirit, this is the way God wants me to live: joyfully, prayerfully, thankfully. I need your help to do so. Desperately. Amen.

33. Come Joyfully

> The Spirit and the bride say, "Come." And
> let everyone who hears say, "Come." And let
> everyone who is thirsty come. Let anyone who
> wishes take the water of life as a gift.
> —REVELATION 22:17

The Spirit of God bids you to come.

The Bride—the beloved of Christ, the church throughout all time, the saints from every place—invites to you come.

And when you come, you are encouraged to turn around and tell others to join you.

You who are parched and dry, come to the Water of Life.

You who are empty and needy, come to fullness.

You who feel burdened and lost, come to rest.

You who desire meaning and purpose, come to fulfillment.

You who seek truth and life, come to joy.

Come and drink deeply and freely and joyfully of the water of life.

This is the invitation of your life. Accept it, and it is yours eternally. Come. Come and drink. Gather around the fountain that will never run dry. The fountain of effervescent spirituality. The fountain of sweet surrender. The fountain of refreshing joy. The fountain of life.

You are invited here. The party is just beginning. Don't be late.

◦◦◦

Holy Spirit, I hear you calling me. I see you beckoning to me. Loosen the shackles of fear and uncertainty that keep me from coming to you. I am thirsty for you. I want to drink freely of the water of life. And live in your joy forever. Amen.

Conclusion

Accepting God's Invitations

Many years ago, when *Braveheart*—the Academy Award-winning film extolling the adventurous virtues of William Wallace, the hero of Scotland—was about to be released, I came up with what I thought was a brilliant idea.

I had noticed in checking the newly released telephone book (remember those?) that there were five other "Peter Wallaces" in the Metro Atlanta area. What a hoot it would be, I thought, to invite the other five Peter Wallaces to meet for an outing to see this movie about the hero who bore our last name. Who knows, maybe we'd become friends and start an exclusive society of Peter Wallaces.

I gathered their addresses from the phone book and worked up an appealing invitation. What fun this would be, I thought. We could compare notes about what it was like living with the name "Peter Wallace"—not that there's anything terribly unique or exciting about it. But still.

I sent out the invitations anticipating the fun we'd have when we would all introduce ourselves to our server at the restaurant before the movie. What a riot!

Days passed. Weeks. The movie finally premiered. And I never heard back from one single other Peter Wallace.

Was my invitation too weird to be taken seriously? Too unusual, unbelievable, or extraordinary? Too unexpected? Too good to be true? Were they all just too busy? Did the other Peter Wallaces *have a life?*

I have no idea. On hindsight, it was a bizarre idea, I'll admit.

I wonder: do we consider God's gracious invitations to us in the same way and fail to take God up on them because they're just too bizarre? Too unusual? Too much?

Throughout scripture, from Genesis to Revelation, God generously beckons us to come closer, to live more authentically, to reach out to others to bring them into the family.

I suspect one of the reasons you picked up this book is that you, like me, are tired of playing the game, of simply going through the motions. You want to be with God. You want to experience a *genuine* spirituality—one that brings fulfillment, purpose, and challenge to your soul. And you want to make a difference in the world for the One who has so graciously and radically transformed you. You want to accept the bold, even unusual invitations God has relentlessly issued to you through the pages of scripture.

A whole lot of people in this world may consider them too unbelievable, too extraordinary, too good to be true. Or they're just too busy to mess with them. But not you. You are ready to go for it.

I think the Apostle Paul felt much the same way. And look how his life and ministry changed the world.

When I was trying to gather my thoughts for this final invitation to you, I discovered Paul had pretty much already said it, much better than I ever could—and with far more authenticity. I hope you'll read, slowly and carefully, the apostle's encouragement to the Philippians to join him in the adventure of authentic Christian living:

> Compared to the high privilege of knowing Christ Jesus as my Master, firsthand, everything I once thought I had going for me is insignificant—dog dung. I've dumped it all in the trash so that I could embrace Christ and be embraced by him. I didn't want some petty, inferior brand of righteousness that comes from keeping a list of rules when I could get the robust kind that comes from trusting Christ—*God's* righteousness.
>
> I gave up all that inferior stuff so I could know Christ personally, experience his resurrection power, be a partner in his suffering, and go all the way with him

to death itself. If there was any way to get in on the resurrection from the dead, I wanted to do it.

I'm not saying that I have this all together, that I have it made. But I am well on my way, reaching out for Christ, who has so wondrously reached out for me. Friends, don't get me wrong: By no means do I count myself an expert in all of this, but I've got my eye on the goal, where God is beckoning us onward—to Jesus. I'm off and running, and I'm not turning back.

So let's keep focused on that goal, those of us who want everything God has for us. If any of you have something else in mind, something less than total commitment, God will clear your blurred vision— you'll see it yet! Now that we're on the right track, let's stay on it.

Stick with me, friends. Keep track of those you see running this same course, headed for this same goal. There are many out there taking other paths, choosing other goals, and trying to get you to go along with them. I've warned you of them many times; sadly, I'm having to do it again. All they want is easy street. They hate Christ's Cross. But easy street is a dead-end street. Those who live there make their bellies their gods; belches are their praise; all they can think of is their appetites.

But there's far more to life for us. We're citizens of high heaven! We're waiting the arrival of the Savior, the Master, Jesus Christ, who will transform our earthy bodies into glorious bodies like his own. He'll make us beautiful and whole with the same powerful skill by which he is putting everything as it should be, under and around him.

My dear, dear friends! I love you so much. I do want the very best for you. You make me feel such joy, fill me with such pride. Don't waver. Stay on track, steady in God (Philippians 3:8—4:1, *The Message*).

Amen!

God is indeed beckoning us onward. Onward to Christ. Onward to sacrificial service. Onward to eternal fulfillment.

God woos us to embrace Jesus and be embraced by him. God coaxes us to keep focused on everything God has for us. God beckons us to live generously in holy love, grace, and power.

It's time to accept these incredible invitations to real life. And enjoy them forever.

Endnotes

[1] Hadith Qudsi 15, quoted by Daisy Kahn in a presentation to the Faith & Values Media Member Council in May 2003. Note that a slightly different version appears in print in *Forty Hadith Qudsi*, edited by Ezzeddin Ibrahim and Denys Johnson-Davies, published by the Islamic Texts Society, Cambridge, England, 1997. However, I prefer the wording Daisy used in her presentation.

[2] Saint Augustine

[3] Adapted from a chapter in *Comstock & Me: My Brief But Unforgettable Career with The West Virginia Hillbilly*, a memoir by the author (2020).

[4] Thich Nhat Hanh, *The Miracle of Mindfulness*, Boston: Beacon Press, 1975-76, p. 4.

[5] Barbara Lundblad, "What the Mighty Might Learn," *Day 1* sermon for February 16, 2003.

[6] Karen Johnson. *Living with Christ*, Vol. 4, No. 8, August 2003, p. 95.

[7] Agnieszka Tennant, "A Shrink Gets Stretched." *Christianity Today*, Vol. 47, No. 5, May 2003, p. 52.

Scripture Index

About the Author

Peter M. Wallace, an Episcopal priest serving in the Diocese of Atlanta, is the executive producer and host of the *Day 1* radio/podcast and internet ministry (Day1.org) and president of the Alliance for Christian Media, based in Atlanta, Georgia. The weekly *Day 1* radio program, the voice of the historic Protestant churches, is distributed to more than 200 radio stations across America and in a dozen other countries.

Peter is the author of 11 other books, including *Getting to Know Jesus (Again): Meditations for Lent*; *Connected: You and God in the Psalms*; and *Living Loved: Knowing Jesus as the Lover of Your Soul*. He has written a memoir, *Comstock & Me: My Brief But Unforgettable Career with The West Virginia Hillbilly* (Amazon). He is also the editor of *Day 1* formation resources, including *Faith and Science in the 21st Century: A Postmodern Primer* and *Bread Enough for All: A Day1 Guide to Life*.

He has contributed to numerous books, sermon resources, study Bibles, devotional books, and magazines. Peter earned a bachelor's degree in journalism from Marshall University and a Master of Theology degree with honors from Dallas Theological Seminary. He completed Episcopal Studies coursework at Candler School of Theology at Emory University.

Peter lives in Atlanta with his spouse, Daniel Le. His website is www.petermwallace.com

About Forward Movement

Forward Movement inspires disciples and empowers evangelists. While we produce great resources like this book, Forward Movement is not a publishing company. We are a discipleship ministry. We live out this ministry through creating and publishing books, daily reflections, studies for small groups, and online resources. People around the world read daily devotions through *Forward Day by Day*, which is also available in Spanish (*Adelante día a día*) and Braille, online, as a podcast, and as an app for smartphones.

We actively seek partners across the church and look for ways to provide resources that inspire and challenge. A ministry of the Episcopal Church since 1935, Forward Movement is a nonprofit organization funded by sales of resources and gifts from generous donors.

To learn more about Forward Movement and our work, visit us at forwardmovement.org or venadelante.org. We are delighted to be doing this work and invite your prayers and support.